"Tommy Bowman is not only an integral part of our program's history, but the qualities he possesses are the same ones we look for in our players today. Driven by faith, Bowman displayed hard work and tenacity to not only become Baylor's first African American scholarship athlete but to excel on and off the floor, weaving himself into the fabric of our basketball program. At Baylor, we talk about Preparing Champions for Life, and I don't think anybody exemplifies a champion in life quite like Tommy."

—**SCOTT DREW**, Head Coach, Baylor University Men's Basketball

"Tommy Bowman is known for being the first Black scholarship athlete at Baylor, but I will always remember him for his integrity, hard work, and character, both on the court and off. I'm honored to have recruited him, to have been his coach, and to have witnessed his impact as a player, friend, husband, and father."

—**CARROLL DAWSON**, former Head Coach, Baylor University Men's Basketball, and former Assistant Coach and General Manager, Houston Rockets

"As much as this book is about sports, it is also a wonderful narrative about Tommy Bowman's display of an unwavering Christian faith that carried him through the racist taunts and slights, even from young children, as he humbly met history as the first Black scholarship athlete at Baylor University. Overshadowed by other Texas sports trailblazers of the 1960s—such as TCU's James Cash, SMU's Jerry Levias, and Baylor football walk-on John Westbrook—Bowman was a gifted basketball player (All-Southwest Conference) and devoted family man whose 'kindness and Christian manner,' as one friend described him, always stood out. Kudos to Chad Conine for expertly weaving this inspiring and long overdue story with a look at Baylor's basketball history."

—**MICHAEL HURD**, author of *Thursday Night Lights: The Story of Black High School Football in Texas*

"The story of Tommy Bowman, first Black scholarship athlete at Baylor University, is a compelling one of commitment, faith, determination, and providence, and it is well told by author Chad Conine. By any standard, Bowman had a successful sports career and was eventually elected to the Southwest Conference Hall of Fame. I never had the opportunity to see Tommy Bowman *play*; I have, however, had the privilege of hearing him *pray*. As chair of deacons, Brother Bowman regularly leads in public prayer at Toliver Baptist Church. When Tommy prays, you feel as though you have been ushered into the very presence of God who is, as Deacon Bowman reminds us, 'worthy' of all praise and honor. *Tommy Bowman: Answering the Call* reveals that Tommy Bowman was a player of exceptional skill and a man of even more extraordinary faith and character—the right person at the right time. This book is a must-read for anyone who wants to understand the history of sports and race at Baylor University."

—**MIKEAL C. PARSONS**, University Distinguished Professor and Macon Chair in Religion, Baylor University

"Chad S. Conine's *Tommy Bowman: Answering the Call* is a work certainly worth reading. Chapter by chapter this inspiring book tells the story of a young man from humble beginnings in Athens, Texas, who had no idea God had a purpose for his life to become the 'first' African American basketball athlete on academic scholarship at Baylor University, Waco. God's providential design has always been the leading force of whom Bowman always gives credit. Because of the door that opened for him, now every person of color in this sport stands on the shoulders of Tommy Bowman, the one who successfully blazed the trail."

—**JIMMY D. HUNTER**, Pastor, Toliver Chapel Missionary Baptist Church

TOMMY BOWMAN

TOMMY BOWMAN

Answering the Call

Chad S. Conine

BIG BEAR BOOKS

Cover design by Virginia Green
Cover image courtesy of Baylor Athletics via the Texas Collection
Book design by Ely Encarnación for Baylor University Press

The Library of Congress has cataloged this book under ISBN
978-1-4813-2003-0.

Library of Congress Control Number: 2023025765

To my Baylor friends

Contents

Acknowledgments

This book began with an email I received from Tommy Bowman's former teammate David Sibley. In it, Sibley asked if I would be interested in writing a book about a local sports figure. We met at a coffee shop in Woodway and Mr. Sibley told me some of Bowman's story. Mr. Sibley and another one of Tommy's close friends, Gary Thomas, were interested in helping to bring a Tommy Bowman biography to fruition. Mr. Sibley and Mr. Thomas helped with the resources and suggestions I needed to get started. In particular, Mr. Sibley recommended I speak with Carroll Dawson as soon as possible.

Coach Dawson, or "CD" as his former players and friends call him, is an author's dream. He is such a good storyteller that any number of books could originate from his anecdotes from a lifetime working in sports.

On the dedication page of this book, I mentioned my Baylor friends. I grew up in Waco as a Red Raider in a foreign land even before I attended Texas Tech in the late 1990s and graduated in August 2000. In better moments, I have understood that sports are supposed to be fun. I've (sometimes) empathized with my Baylor-fan friends as they have experienced success and failure (again in my better moments) over the last three decades. The list could probably run on for several pages, but I'll venture to single out Jeremy Webb, Dave and Woody Rogers, Brent Baker, Bob Johns, Ronny Higgins, Tommy

Ross, Cliff Smith, Dave Deaconson, Shawn Skeen, Blake Boyd, Hank Steen, Greg Moss, Trey Hagins, Bruce Cotharn, Josh Blake, Brad and Brent Wilson, Tye Barrett, David Crowder, Jacob Robinson, and Alex Cox. Even in writing this, I sense that I have left out some important names. But they are all represented here.

Writing about sports history is much easier for me than following sports in real time. My mom and dad, John and Shana Conine, almost always get a call from me when our team wins. Our family are Red Raiders, and that includes my sister Chaney Cockrell, her husband Ian, and their kids, Eli, Evan, and Ella. My sister Calley Durant is officially a Horned Frog, but her husband Wes and daughter Reagan sympathize with the red and black (actually, I don't think Reagan really cares too much, for which I admire her).

I've been blessed to work with some fantastic, award-winning sportswriters through the years. Among them, Brice Cherry, John Werner, Jason Orts, Kim Gorum, Jerry Hill, and David G. Campbell have been consistent friends as well as colleagues for many years now. Legendary *Waco Trib* sports editor Dave Campbell was also a good friend and constant inspiration.

Longtime *Waco Trib* photo editor Rod Aydelotte assisted with converting some of the photos for this book. Rod is the hardest working person I know and is also an articulate sender of text messages. *Waco Trib* photographer Jerry Larson also helped with some photo conversions.

Ultimately, this project could not have come together without Tommy Bowman's help. He and his family told me their stories in an open, honest, and humble way that made it very easy for me to turn them into a cohesive narrative. Tommy, Krystal, Tommy II, and Jackie, along with a few extended family members, were all gracious in speaking with me, and I hope I was able to represent their story well.

✦ ✦ ✦

A note on sources: The research for *Tommy Bowman: Answering the Call* was built on two main journalistic sources—interviews and newspaper archives.

I interviewed eighteen individuals and compiled more than 25,000 words of interview transcripts. I began by speaking with Carroll Dawson, who was a tremendous asset not only in telling his and Tommy's intersecting stories, but also in pointing me in the direction of Baylor's in-house mini-documentary, "Tommy Bowman's Story," which can be viewed on YouTube under the heading "Baylor Basketball (M): Tommy Bowman Feature" and was produced by Brooke Bednarz for Baylor Athletics. It served as an introduction to Tommy Bowman's place in Baylor history.

The majority of my newspaper archives research was completed at the West Waco Library & Genealogy Center. The library maintains copies of the *Waco News Tribune*, *Waco Times Herald*, and *Waco Tribune-Herald* microfilms. This was a valuable source in reading first-hand accounts of Bowman's teams at Baylor filed by sportswriters Jim Montgomery, Hollis Biddle, Dave Campbell, and others.

I also used the online newspaper archives of the Fort Worth Public Library to read *Fort Worth Star-Telegram* stories, in particular about James Cash's TCU teams. And in order to get a balanced account of the Baylor-Texas A&M riot game in 1969, I used the *Bryan Eagle* microfilms located at the Carnegie History Center in Bryan, Texas.

Painting a reliable and accurate picture of American culture in the 1960s required careful online research. A couple of the more valuable sources included "A Look Back at 1967" by the *Atlantic*, and "A Timeline of 1968" at Smithsonianmag.com.

As related to sports in the South, Charles Martin's "Benching Jim Crow" was a very useful source of information. I also was able to get a fair look at Texas A&M's evolution as a campus from the article "Celebrating Black History and Achievements at Texas A&M" at tamu.edu. Similarly, I used an essay titled "An Institution in Slow Motion" from blogs.baylor.edu.

The Texas Collection library on the Baylor campus provided many of the photos used in this book, and they are credited with the photos. The Texas Collection also contained Baylor Basketball press guides from the late 1960s and early 1970s where I was able to find relevant stats and verify details that had been shared with me in interviews.

On the subject of Baylor media guides, Baylor basketball's program almanac is, in a way, an evolving document. Many versions of it can be accessed at baylorbears.com, and they are updated annually. I used the 2020–21 version as a guide for dates as I looked up specific games of the Bowman era in newspaper archives. I reached out to Matt Roberts, Baylor men's basketball director of communications, to verify at least one all-time list point of fact. And in one instance, I found a statistical record that needed updating that I passed along to Mr. Roberts.

James Cash, along with supplying his biographical information, pointed me in the direction of a mini-documentary titled "Stories of the PVIL." It gave descriptions of I. M. Terrell High School, the formation of Cash's friendship with Garvin Isaacs, Cash's senior season playing for Robert Hughes, and Cash's recruitment to TCU.

Mr. Sibley passed along to me audio and video accounts of the "Riot at College Station," which I used to add details about that most memorable game.

Finally, the Bowman family passed along photos and other useful clips and accounts from their family collection. I believe these helped give the most accurate account I could write in this book, and I hope that I've done it well.

Members of Baylor's 1966–67 freshman team—(from left) David Sibley,
Carroll Dawson (coach), Tommy Bowman, David Croucher, Ernie
Armstrong, Danny Elam, and Larry Gatewood—pose with a commemorative
team picture/plaque at a Baylor game at the Ferrell Center.

Courtesy of the Bowman Family

Introduction

On a mid-July afternoon, in the middle of a long, hot, dry summer in 2022, Tommy Bowman met with some of his former Baylor teammates at a cafe in Huntsville, Texas. The group of old friends—most of them over six feet tall and all of them in their seventies—reunited in a casual restaurant's air-conditioned dining room. They joked with each other and daydreamed about the best possible outcome of a lottery ticket that one of them had just purchased. Outside, a brief but much-needed shower drenched the parking lot, sidewalk, and grass along Sam Houston Avenue. The lifelong buddies caught up for an hour or more while eating chicken fried steak and drinking iced tea.

They were meeting just to meet. Just to see each other. I had been invited as an afterthought. Not wanting to be intrusive, I showed up about an hour and a half after they sat down. Everyone had long since finished eating. They were well on to the storytelling part of the day. I was there to meet and informally interview some of the members of Baylor's basketball teams of the late 1960s.

Bowman politely excused himself. He and Tom Stanton, who had traveled together down from Waco, got up. They shook hands and headed home. I was working on this book and had already recorded several long and revelatory interviews with Bowman. He was gracious, and he told me as much as he could remember. But he didn't want to be present when I asked his old friends about him.

As he and Stanton traveled back to Waco, Bowman confessed to his buddy, "I don't know why they're doing this."

This is the story of an ordinary man who has lived a life into his mid-seventies by simple principles with steadfast conviction. He has not sought attention, and he has successfully avoided it most of the time. And yet his closest friends want his story to be told. More than that, as Baylor University's basketball program prepares to open a new arena, necessitated by the championships of its men's and women's teams, Tommy Bowman's former teammates want to see a statue of him going up along with the new stadium. That is how much they esteem what he did for Baylor and who he is.

So, I am writing a biography of a man who does not even have a Wikipedia page. Tommy Bowman is not famous. He can walk into any store or restaurant in Waco, Texas without attracting too much attention, though his wife, Jackie, regularly sees how his accomplishments on the basketball court resonate with some people in the community. "Anywhere we still go, he's still got to stop and talk, and people remember," Jackie Bowman said. "Tommy might say, 'I don't remember them.' But they remember him, and they talk about certain plays."

Bowman is a tall and slender gentleman with white hair and a beard that give him a distinguished countenance. He spent a brief part of his life in the spotlight, although it was not one he actively pursued. He spent most of his life as a hard-working and dutiful administrator in the trucking business as well as an equally dutiful and hard-working husband and father. He and Jackie have been married for more than fifty years. They have two children, Tommy II and Krystal, and four grandchildren. His kids are hard workers too but, like their father, not famous.

Bowman is a normal guy on the surface. However, if national championship-winning Baylor basketball coach Scott Drew spotted Bowman in a Waco restaurant, I'm certain Drew would stop by and offer a handshake and an appreciative smile. Coach Drew has come over to say hi to me at a pizza place, and I'm just a sportswriter. Bowman was a pioneer for the Baylor basketball program as its first African American scholarship athlete. He withstood the storms of hostile arenas and endured the quiet challenge of fitting in amid an almost exclusively white, mostly affluent university campus. It was less than one hundred miles from his hometown of Athens, Texas but culturally a world away from where he grew up.

Bowman didn't flinch.

He showed up and did the things he was asked to do. He competed on the basketball court as hard as he could. He maintained his integrity and treated people the way he wanted to be treated. As a result, Bowman is the type of man who is prominent in the minds of people who are much more acclaimed than him.

Before coming to Baylor, he was a small-town kid headed for a small-town type of life in rural East Texas. Bowman, a committed Christian since his days as a boy in the pew next to his grandmother, believes the Lord intervened and put him on a different path.

"God has blessed me in so many ways that I couldn't even begin to tell you. To come from Athens, living in Pine Grove, I can remember one of my greatest thrills was to be out there in the country on a dirt road, running by a casing, what we called the casing," Bowman said. "It was a tire. We'd just take a tire and start rolling it. We didn't have anything to play with. I can remember having so much joy about that. I can remember looking back on it and thinking, 'What the heck made me so happy about running behind a tire?' I know everything is relative, but God has brought me such a long way. Sometimes I think about it and get emotional thinking about how good He is and how blessed my wife and I are."

Seemingly in a day's time, Bowman was thrust into the role of trailblazer. Without trying to, perhaps even without consciously deciding to do it, Bowman became the first Black scholarship athlete at Baylor University and the second African American basketball player in the now-extinct Southwest Conference.

In four years at Baylor, Bowman set himself apart on the basketball court, twice earning all conference first-team honors as well as Southwest Conference Sophomore of the Year in 1968. That accomplishment made headlines in the sports pages. But more quietly, Bowman established himself in his studies at Baylor. He quickly found out he could compete in the gym with his teammates. Even before practice began, he showed what he could do in pick-up games with the men who would become his closest friends. But gaining the confidence to speak up or answer questions in lectures took more time. That was the hard work and the hard-won victory that Bowman believes paid off bigger in the end.

He hardly flirted with a professional basketball career. Soon after graduating from Baylor, he went to work as a manager in the freight industry—a hardscrabble business full of crusty, rugged white men. But he had the combination of intellect and toughness to thrive in a variety of roles.

To him, that's his legacy.

As the Baylor basketball program has moved into the highest level of national prominence, Bowman's teammates and friends want his story to be known because they realize that their own stories alongside him were so much more important than they knew at the time. As I mentioned earlier, some of them are pushing for a Tommy Bowman statue to be included in the plans for the school's new basketball arena. It will never happen if Bowman has any say in it.

Baylor has honored Bowman in a variety of ways throughout the decades since he broke the color barrier at the school in men's basketball. He's in the Baylor University Athletics Hall of Fame, and he represented the Bears as an inductee to the Southwest Conference Hall of Fame. But he's unaffected by those honors.

"He was a trustee at Baylor with (David) Sibley and Drayton McLane and all those people. He's a champion on so many fronts. Not enough accolades can be given," Stanton said. "But when they come, Tommy will go over in the corner and sheepishly shuffle his feet and can't hardly wait for it to be over."

This is Bowman's story. It includes the stories of a lot of the people around him: the coach who signed him, the teammates who embraced and stood by him, and a competitor and friend and fellow pioneer. They're all important and have stories of their own. They added to his experience, but they didn't necessarily shape it. His character was forged as a young man as he learned the Sunday school values insisted upon by his mother, grandmother, and grandfather. He refused to waver from them.

He simply answered the call.

1965

On Sunday, March 7, 1965, civil rights activist John Lewis led a march that was intended to begin in Selma, Alabama and travel along US Route 80 to the state capitol in Montgomery in support of equal voting rights for Black citizens in the state. As the 600 marchers were crossing the Edmund Pettus Bridge in Selma, they could see Alabama state troopers blocking Route 80 on the south side of the Alabama River.

Following a brief standoff during which the marchers remained peaceful but refused to disperse, they were attacked by the state troopers. The violent scenes that commenced received national news coverage. Photographs of Lewis being beaten and of marcher and activist Amelia Boynton lying unconscious circulated in daily newspapers throughout the United States. The *Waco News Tribune* ran the story atop the front page with the headline, "Bedlam in Selma after Police Break Up March," and the article included a centerpiece photo of troopers attacking the crowd.

The events at the Edmund Pettus Bridge became known as "Bloody Sunday" and struck an emphatic chord in the crescendo of the civil rights movement.

At that time, the athletic programs in both the Southwest Conference and Southeastern Conference—made up of schools in Texas, Arkansas, Louisiana, Mississippi, Alabama, Florida, Georgia, Tennessee, and Kentucky—remained segregated.

That was about to change in Texas.

In the spring of 1965, Southern Methodist University football coach Hayden Fry offered a football scholarship to Jerry LeVias from Beaumont while Texas Christian University basketball coach Buster Brannon extended a basketball scholarship offer to James Cash of Fort Worth's I. M. Terrell High School.

Cash said he and LeVias have had an ongoing debate through the years about which one of them signed first. Whatever the case, their paths are connected and, in Cash's mind, linked to the events in Alabama.

"TCU made the offer just a few days after the Edmund Pettus Bridge, where they were marching across in Selma," Cash said. "That was just a few weeks before I actually signed. 'Bloody Sunday' is what they call it. My sense is that was catalytic really in the Southwest Conference for some of the schools."

Baylor University was close behind SMU and TCU. As the 1966–67 school year began, walk-on football player John Westbrook was preparing to suit up for the Bears and join LeVias as the first Black football players in the SWC (both LeVias and Westbrook were sophomores who, like all student athletes at the time, were not eligible for varsity competition as freshmen). Meanwhile, Tommy Bowman moved into Martin Hall and started his college career as Baylor's first African American scholarship athlete.

1
Once Upon a Time in Athens, Texas

The video montage of the 1960s, as played in the collective imagination of the twenty-first century, is all drama and action, protests and violence, and culture exploding everywhere. Martin Luther King Jr., John F. Kennedy, Muhammad Ali, The Beatles, Jimi Hendrix, Malcolm X, and John Wooden all played leading roles as the world seemed to change from one thing in 1959 to something totally different by 1970. The 1960s as a decade symbolize cultural upheaval and social change in the twentieth century. Bob Dylan described it succinctly and prophetically as early as 1963 when he recorded "The Times They Are A-Changin'": "you better start swimmin' or you'll sink like a stone."

Driving in his tan Chevy Impala SS on the 143-mile trip from Waco to his hometown of Alba, Texas, Carroll Dawson wanted to be swimming, but really, he was starting to sink. On the surface, Dawson was just a normal guy, driving a normal car on a normal winter day. It was one of those afternoons that might've been forgotten before the week was over. Dawson, Baylor's twenty-eight-year-old freshman team coach and assistant to head basketball coach Bill Menefee, was just making a quick trip home to see his mother.

Baylor's varsity basketball team was in the middle of a disappointing eight-win, sixteen-loss season. The Bears went 6–8 in Southwest Conference play and tied for sixth. But no alarms were sounding. Menefee had coached Baylor to one winning campaign in five years at the school. His overall record included forty-one wins and seventy-nine losses. It didn't bother many people though. The SWC was a football conference, after all. Basketball was fun, but nonessential. People liked Menefee and weren't in a hurry to get rid of him.

Dawson, though, wanted to win. He was the fiery competitive complement to Menefee's calm, intellectual demeanor. Dawson was also in charge of recruiting. He excelled at it. But by the early part of 1966 he had given up on the revolution at hand, at least as it applied to the current recruiting cycle. Two years earlier, Baylor athletic director/head football coach John Bridgers told Dawson to be ready to sign an African American scholarship athlete in basketball. Bridgers believed the school's first Black student athlete should be a basketball player because he would be more visible, not covered up by a football helmet and pads. There was one problem. Most Southwest Conference schools had resisted integration in intercollegiate athletics. Whether it was a back-room agreement, an unspoken understanding, or a decided-upon policy of the various university boards of regents, none of the SWC schools had allowed Black student athletes prior to 1965.

As 1965 progressed, that was changing, though slowly and sporadically. SMU football coach Hayden Fry signed Jerry LeVias, a wide receiver from Beaumont's Hebert High School, in the spring. At the time, freshmen were not eligible to play on the varsity squad in football or men's basketball. LeVias also battled injuries during his freshman season, so his arrival in the SWC had not yet caused ripples. TCU basketball coach Buster Brannon signed James Cash from nearby Fort Worth's I. M. Terrell High School the same spring that Fry inked LeVias. Dawson coached his Baylor freshman team against the six-foot-six Cash in SWC play during the 1966 basketball season.

Ironically, as Dawson traveled from Waco to Alba, a Texas university was about to make history. Texas Western, which was not a member of the SWC, had integrated its basketball program in the 1950s, but it took Don Haskins to make the school famous. Haskins, who started his coaching tenure at Texas Western in 1961, recruited talent from all over the country and created a diverse Miners roster. He guided Texas Western to the NCAA Final Four in 1966, where his team defeated Utah in the national semifinals. The win over the Utes put Texas Western in a national championship game that came with a glaring spotlight. The Miners faced legendary Kentucky coach Adolph Rupp and his all-white Wildcats. Haskins took the bait, starting five Black players in the championship game—Bobby Joe Hill, David Lattin, Orsten Artis, Nevil Shedd, and Harry Flourney.

Texas Western beat Kentucky, 72–65, in one of the most famous outcomes of the long and storied history of the NCAA Men's Basketball Tournament. It inspired the film *Glory Road* forty years later and stood for five and a half decades as the state of Texas's only national championship in Division I men's college basketball.

Dawson, keenly aware of Haskins's success and the changing landscape, was prepared to integrate Baylor. Although the basketball program had very little money to spend on recruiting, he had identified prospects and was ready to make a move in 1964 and 1965. But Bridgers and Baylor, taking the temperature of the SWC (or perhaps the school's own decision-makers), wouldn't give the green light.

"The third year, which was Tommy's year, I told Mr. Bridgers, 'We're wasting money. We don't have it. I'm not going to waste a lot of money this year,'" Dawson recalled. "I didn't do anything, and they passed the rule (allowing Black student athletes)."

The Baylor assistant coach knew he was falling behind when he pulled into a gas station in Athens, Texas on that fateful day in the winter of 1966. A gas station attendant in his mid-forties walked up to the Impala and noticed the Baylor parking sticker on the windshield. Granville Crayton was the observant type, and, on that day, he was an agent of change.

Crayton asked about the Baylor sticker. Dawson said he was a basketball coach, which was the exact answer Crayton wanted to hear.

"We've got the best basketball player in the state right here in Athens," Crayton said.

For some reason, Dawson's ears perked up.

Dawson's father, Julie Dawson, owned and operated a service station in Alba when Carroll was growing up. He spent a lot of days there and knew how much information passed from one source to another with the station attendants serving as middlemen. They were in the know in an era long before twenty-four-hour news channels, Twitter, or Internet message boards.

It's hard to imagine a major college basketball coach paying heed to the mention of a talented player from someone he just met by chance. Maybe that's because of the massive recruiting machine that has taken over modern athletics. In the information age, a college basketball recruiter can sift through lists of prospects in a matter of seconds, instantly finding key data points on players as young as thirteen. They see them at camps and high-profile travel-ball tournaments. The athletes themselves can upload their highlights from their smartphones on the ride home from games. A player whose name isn't known by the start of his senior season in high school should mentally prepare for post-basketball life.

Even in 1966, Crayton's claim that Athens was home to the state's best basketball player was a Hail Mary.

Tommy Bowman was the name Crayton gave to Dawson. The Baylor assistant coach just happened to have his recruiting database—a cardboard box full of lists, pamphlets, and questionnaires—on the back seat of his Impala. Dawson was just curious enough to look through the box and see what he knew about Tommy Bowman from Athens High School.

Nothing.

Bowman's name wasn't on any of the lists. Dawson didn't know Edward Evans, the head basketball coach at Athens High School. And Evans hadn't bothered to promote Bowman's ability to SWC recruiters.

To be fair, Evans hadn't known Bowman for that long. Bowman grew up attending the Black schools in Athens, including Fisher

High School in ninth, tenth, and eleventh grade. When Athens High School integrated at the start of the 1965–66 school year, Bowman enrolled along with a couple dozen of his classmates from Fisher.

"The first day we arrived on campus, they had written on the side of the walls 'Niggers go home,'" Bowman remembers.

It was jarring, but it didn't stop him.

"We were seniors and we had thirty-something (Black students) in our class. Because I played sports, I think that helped my situation," Bowman said. "When you're on a team, you're on a team. Black, white, whatever. It was not difficult, except you didn't expect to see that written on the side of the wall."

Bowman was a six-foot-four forward on the Athens basketball team. He also played backup quarterback and defensive end in football. He was the type of player that did what his coaches asked for the sake of the team. He didn't cause problems, nor did he stand out (at least in his own mind). He was the same person on the athletic field that he was at home. Bowman's maternal grandmother, Willie Mae Bowman, insisted that he attend Sunday School and church every Sunday morning and go to Baptist Training Union meetings on Sunday night. So that's what he did.

They told Bowman he would be going to Athens High School as a senior, so that's what he did. And it didn't take him long to see there was an upside.

"At the Black high school, they didn't furnish us with tennis shoes. They didn't furnish us with anything except a jersey and shorts. When I went to Athens High School, that was the first time I'd ever had Converse (shoes)," he said. "They gave me a brand new pair of Converse. I thought I'd died and gone to heaven. Before practice every day, you'd go in and get a clean jock, clean pair of shorts, and a clean jersey. At Fisher, we had to provide our own stuff. It was so different."

As his senior basketball season progressed without any playoff fanfare or much else to distinguish Bowman or the Hornets, his plan was to possibly play basketball for two more years at the junior college level.

Bowman believes it was God's hand that moved Granville Crayton to tell Carroll Dawson that the best basketball player in the state lived in the small East Texas town.

"This was providential because I didn't make any all-state team. I didn't make any all-district team. I didn't make any of those," Bowman said. "I don't know why Mr. Granville decided to tell Dawson that he had the best basketball player in the state of Texas there in Athens. But he did. And that's why I say it was providential."

The divine intervention that prompted Crayton to brag on Bowman kept flowing through Dawson. Despite having no information on the Athens player in his recruiting materials, the Baylor assistant coach decided to extend his stay.

"I don't know what made me get in the car and go down that road," Dawson said.

The Baylor coach asked where Bowman lived. Crayton pointed him just down the road to the house of Mr. George Barker, Tommy's stepfather. Dawson found Bowman's mother, Irene Barker, sitting on the front porch shucking peas. Bowman wasn't home, so Dawson sat down with Mrs. Barker and began helping with the shucking and selling the Bears basketball program.

In 2021, while Baylor's basketball team was on its way to winning the national championship, the school's athletic department produced a mini-documentary on Bowman. It begins with the story of Dawson's pitch to Bowman's mother.

"He sold her, and if I had not come to Baylor, I think she probably would've kicked me out of the house," Bowman said in the documentary with a joking, knowing gleam in his eye.

Dawson had not seen Bowman play basketball. He'd never even met the senior in high school. But he was inspired to make the young man Baylor's first African American scholarship athlete.

"The Good Lord was on my shoulder or something," Dawson said.

In the moment, however, there was the small hangup that Dawson had no idea if Crayton's claim was true. If he was the best basketball player in the state of Texas, then why hadn't he made anyone's recruiting list? Why had Baylor not heard from the Athens High School coach? By the time Bowman was a sophomore and eligible to play on the Bears' varsity squad, Dawson and Menefee knew him to be a versatile six-foot-four athlete with a penchant for rebounding and tough defense.

But Dawson didn't have much to go on while he was shucking peas with Mrs. Barker. Tommy came home that night to learn that he had been successfully recruited to at least visit Baylor. Then Dawson made plans to watch Bowman play. The Baylor coach drove the rest of the way to his mother's house in Alba, then returned to Athens for a game.

It didn't take long for Dawson to see that Bowman was going to fit in just fine in the Southwest Conference.

"I thought, 'Holy cow, how lucky am I?'" Dawson said.

Despite the fact that Dawson found Bowman in relative anonymity in Athens, and even though secrets were easier to keep in the days long before 247Sports or Rivals.com, the contagiousness of college athletics recruiting still took effect after the Bears offered a scholarship. TCU sent an airplane, perhaps to woo Bowman with the opportunity to make his first flight, and brought him a little more than one hundred miles back to the Horned Frogs' campus.

It's possible that Texas A&M coach Shelby Metcalf wanted to sign Bowman too. Tommy's mother had become friends with Metcalf's sister, who lived in Athens, through catering work. But Texas A&M had only recently allowed women to enroll in the school in 1963. Metcalf told Mrs. Barker that the school just wasn't ready for Tommy.

It didn't matter, though—Bowman was all but signed up to go to Baylor by the time he arrived home and found Dawson helping Mrs. Barker prepare the evening meal. In the span of a few hours and thanks to a serendipitous conversation at a gas station by the highway, the lives of both Dawson and Bowman had been altered.

Just as he had been faithful to follow his grandmother's instructions, showing up for church multiple times each week, he was going to honor his mother's wishes and head off to Waco to attend the Baptist, almost completely white Baylor University.

"There were a lot of guys at Fisher High School that were better basketball players than me," Bowman said. "That's why I say it was the providence of God. He intended me to be the first Black scholarship athlete at Baylor. There's not much I can do in the way of taking credit for it."

Tommy Bowman and his mother, Irene Barker.

Courtesy of the Bowman Family

2
Tommy Goes to College

As can happen to anyone who embarks on something that is at once exciting, stressful, and intimidating, Tommy Bowman and his family had a bit of a false start.

Not only was Bowman the first person in his family to go to college, but he was also headed off to an integrated college in late August of 1966. In his hometown of Athens, the occasion prompted a celebration, as everyone knew Tommy was going to Baylor. He would be the school's first Black scholarship athlete, although that wasn't foremost on the minds of all of his friends and family. Bowman said his grandmother, for one, was somewhat indifferent to his basketball career, and he doesn't even know if she was aware of his status as a college sports pioneer.

He loaded up the car with his mother and stepfather, then they drove the ninety or so miles southwest to Waco. But a problem became apparent when they got to the Baylor campus and found locked doors. Bowman's parents misinterpreted the move-in instructions they had received and showed up a week early. Attempting to sort out the glitch, they contacted the dorm director, who showed up and just shrugged it off. Martin Hall, which would be Bowman's home in Waco for the next year, wouldn't be open for another week.

More than fifty years later, Bowman still shakes his head in bemused exasperation.

"Here I am. I've told everybody in Athens that I'm going off to school, and now I've got to go back," he said. "I thought, 'If I have to go back to Athens, I'm just going to stay in the house all week long.'"

That remains as Bowman's most poignant memory of the physical move from his hometown to Baylor University. Eventually, he did get settled into the dorm with roommate Tommy Reaux, another Black student who began life at the school as a walk-on football player. Reaux, an offensive lineman, and teammate John Westbrook, a running back, were both walk-ons who would eventually be granted scholarships. Westbrook was the Bears' first Black athlete to take the field in a varsity game when he played against Syracuse on September 10, 1966.

Almost as soon as Bowman got unpacked in his new room, he headed for Marrs McLean Gym to play some hoops. He was by himself as he walked, but he wasn't alone in his intentions. Even before he exited the dorm to make the short walk down Fifth Street, he noticed two other guys going in the same direction. One was a lanky six-foot-five, the other a compact five-foot-ten.

"And I thought, 'That looks like Mutt and Jeff,'" Bowman said. "I didn't know who they were, they didn't know who I was. I was behind them."

While Bowman was sizing them up, they were doing the same thing. The taller David Sibley and the shorter David Croucher came through high school playing integrated summer league games in Houston. Sibley said the games in Marrs McLean with his future Baylor teammates were nothing compared to the battles he'd seen in his hometown gym.

"We wondered. I didn't know who they'd signed," Sibley said. "I think we passed (Bowman), and after we were away from him we said, 'I wonder if that's a basketball player.' I hadn't seen a team picture. He was tall and looked fit. We knew they had one Black football player. He was too tall to be that guy."

At that moment, Bowman was in a new situation, one where he had to adapt to the culture on a college campus in a bigger city than the one where he had grown up. This wasn't like going into Athens

High School on the first day of his senior year with thirty other Black students. Nor did it have the official structure of high school basketball. Pick-up basketball games are played in a world of absolute meritocracy. If you can play, you can stay. If you can't, you find out pretty quick.

+ + +

Tommy Bowman was born on May 9, 1948, in Athens, Texas. He was never close to his father. He took his mother's maiden name, so he has the same surname as his maternal grandmother and grandfather, Willie Mae and Gaston Bowman.

In the early years, Tommy lived close with his extended family. Very close. Madea, the kids' name for Willie Mae, and Daddy Gaston's house in Pine Grove, just south of Athens, had three bedrooms and a kitchen. Tommy's Aunt Lynda, who is two years younger than him and whom he calls Poochie, said she remembers a fourth bedroom but can't recall where it was and thinks it's possibly just her imagination. Tommy's mother Irene had a twin sister, Fayrene, and they both lived at home, as did their children. Willie Mae and Gaston also had younger children: Lynda and her older sister, Alice, who was the same age as Tommy. Tommy has an older sister named Johnny, and Fayrene had a son named William, who was Tommy's age.

Tommy, William, Alice, and Lynda were a unit, a social circle, a family within a family.

"And happy as a lark, we were," Lynda said. "We had company all the time. There were always people coming to visit and some of our friends coming out to spend the night. Sometimes we would make a pallet out on the front porch. We had this huge front porch.

"We were just country kids, but it was wonderful. If I could do any of that over again, I don't think I would change a thing. I think it just made us into the people that we are now. Some pretty good human beings."

The Bowman kids spent part of their days doing chores like hauling water in from the well in the front yard. The house didn't have running water. They also collected wood and kindling for the fireplace. And then they spent part of their days just being kids. Bowman described rolling a tire down a dirt road. Lynda added that they would take cardboard boxes and slide down a dirt hill not far from the house.

Lynda has fond memories of Willie Mae getting up early before anyone else, turning on the heater, and making breakfast. They would wake up to the smell of sausage frying and biscuits baking. Homemade breakfast was just the start of the daily routine for Madea.

"She cooked breakfast, lunch, and dinner," Lynda said. "We'd walk home from school at lunch and go back to school with a full tummy and then come home to a different meal for dinner.

"She could stretch. Tommy says, 'I don't know how Madea could take one chicken and we would all eat.' The eight of us would eat off that one chicken and everybody was full. You couldn't ask for another piece because there wasn't any more. But we all had our favorite piece of the chicken. Tommy and William had the side piece. Alice and I had the wings. My mother always got the back and the neck. I didn't understand at the time why she chose the back and the neck. But as I became older and became a mother, I realized that mothers do what they have to do for their children. They take the least popular pieces with the least amount of meat on them."

While Willie Mae took care of the house and prepared three meals a day for the entire family, Gaston went to work. He was a bricklayer during the day. But when he got home from that job, he went directly to side jobs, mowing lawns and feeding hogs for farmers in the area.

"He was a busy, busy man that didn't mind working," Lynda said "He had kids to feed. We all just adored him, and we still talk a lot about Daddy. We have some sweet memories of him."

She also said Gaston was the only man that Tommy ever called Daddy. Gaston and his brothers were tall, lean men, and that seems to be where Tommy got his basketball physique.

Irene married George Barker when Tommy was in the second grade. About that time, they moved into a house in the Black neighborhood on the north side of Athens. Not long after that, Willie Mae and Gaston moved into a house next door, and Fayrene and her family lived just up the street.

Of course, it was a time of separate but definitely not equal, especially in East Texas. There were certain places in town they weren't allowed to go. They couldn't swim at the community pool, for one thing.

Asked if there was a Black newspaper in town, Bowman just chuckled. He said there were no Black businesses in Athens that he could remember. He and his family found enough work to make ends meet. "We depended on the white man for everything," he said. They had community, but they didn't have the kind of Black society that was present in larger cities in 1960s America.

Even so, there was a basketball goal in the neighborhood and Bowman spent many of his days playing games with friends and practicing on his own.

"When we'd get through playing, I had certain shots I had to make and I had to make them all consecutively," Bowman said. "A free throw, a jump shot from the top of the key, all of that. I would not go in the house until I made all of them. I remember and think, 'Why did I do that?' I never considered myself a basketball player. There were three or four guys that were better than me. They were older than me."

Basketball helped him fit in at school, both at Fisher High School and then at Athens High after it was integrated. However, it wasn't always his identity. In junior high, he made the "B" team and distinctly recalls how he and his classmates pooled their resources on game days. It was a fact of life at the Black junior high and high school that everyone had to find a way to do more with less. After he played in the "B" team game, he would take off his sneakers and loan them to a member of the "A" team. Bowman still recalls and is still a little repulsed by just how sweaty they were when he would eventually get those sneakers back.

By the time he was in tenth grade, Bowman had progressed on the basketball court. He made the varsity squad as a sophomore. He still didn't strut around thinking he was God's basketball gift to the school, though. He said a teammate, Robert Johnson, was the tallest kid on the team and therefore the dominant post. A player named Abe Rhinehart had the most talent.

When Bowman was old enough to get odd jobs in the summer, he came into closer contact with racial discrimination. One summer day is particularly burned in his memory. He had been hired to help load watermelons onto a truck so they could be hauled into Athens and sold in the town square. He did his part and then went to get his money for an afternoon's work.

"I remember the guy was sitting on the ground—a big, burly white guy. When he paid me, he got the money and determined how much he owed me, and he just threw it on the ground," Bowman said. "That kind of epitomizes what we went through over there in Athens at the time."

While there were hard lessons and painful realities about how Black people were treated, and few if any perks to growing up Black in a small East Texas town, there was an upside to Bowman's close-knit community. Willie Mae made sure Tommy went to church any-time the doors were open. She insisted on it and didn't take excuses. Bowman followed orders even when he wanted to buck against Madea's rules. He was baptized the summer before seventh grade. All that time in church made an indelible impression on Bowman.

"I understand now that she did it because she loved me," he said. "I'm so glad that she did."

Going from high school to college wasn't an established path for Bowman's family or for anyone in the community where he grew up. He figured he had enough skills on the court to perhaps make the local junior college team and therefore continue playing sports to earn a few more academic credits.

As a senior he helped Athens High win nineteen games while losing only eight. Lynda said everyone in the school knew Tommy was a great basketball player, even if he didn't self-identify as such. She also said his tall, lean frame and good looks made him a lightning rod for girls' attention. "But he was never the playboy type, even though he could've been," Lynda said. "He was a one-woman man, even back then."

The Athens basketball team was good with Bowman quietly leading the way.[*] But they were not quite good enough for lasting glory. In an era when the bar to make the playoffs was much higher in Texas high school athletics than it is now, the Hornets fell short of the postseason. Their final game of the campaign was a 69–45 defeat of Terrell High, but two losses to Waxahachie left Athens in second place.

Bowman could have easily faded into anonymity, but Carroll Dawson took a chance.

"I met Dawson. I came home, and he was sitting on the porch shelling peas with my mama," Bowman said. "I thought, 'Who is this white boy?'"

Dawson couldn't keep Bowman a secret. Word got out to TCU and Oklahoma that the Athens senior was a legitimate prospect. In Fort Worth, Horned Frogs coach Buster Brannon told James Cash that Bowman was the best player in Texas in the class of 1966. When TCU sent an airplane to pick up Bowman and bring him back to the big city, it might have actually been a mistake.

"Waco was more suited for me, being from Athens, than being in a metropolitan area like Fort Worth or Dallas," Bowman said. "I was intimidated by big schools."

For his official visit to Baylor, Dawson drove Bowman from Athens to Waco in the coach's Chevy SuperSport Impala. Obviously, Dawson took advantage of his captive audience on the two-hour drive to keep pitching the school, the Bears' basketball team, and his and head coach Bill Menefee's program for player development.

"Dawson says, 'Tommy, you're going to be a good college player. But there are a few weaknesses that you have. If you come

---

[*]   Author's note: During the wrapping up of this project, Bowman found a newspaper article that stated he averaged 26.7 points a game and ranked in the top quarter of his class academically.

to Baylor, I'll help you work through those weaknesses,'" Bowman remembered. "That's the last time I heard it was in the car on the way back. I think it was just one of those come-on things. If I come to Baylor, Coach Dawson will help make me a better player."

Bowman formed a bond with Cash on his trip to Fort Worth, and they would remain friends through their college years. But Dawson had convinced Irene Barker that he would look after her son. In turn, Bowman was going to follow his mother's wishes. In that sense, Bowman was committed to Baylor before he even considered going to the school.

The world is full of people who won't do anything that they didn't think of themselves. The desire for independence of thought and action is a powerful force. There's also a massive swath of the population that just goes with the flow without too much creativity or initiative.

Bowman possessed the ability to follow instructions, especially from people he trusted, such as his mother, grandmother, and grandfather. At the same time, he could act on his own discernment and instincts. The latter came into play when he set off on his own in Waco.

+   +   +

Once he moved into his dorm room, it was time to start figuring out how the basketball piece was going to fit. Bowman went directly to the gym, carrying with him all of the excitement and nervousness that go along with discovering what you're made of. He walked into a gym that was full of athletes who had been in that environment plenty of times before, guys who had been playing pick-up ball in big city games for years.

"What you've got to understand is I'm from Athens, Texas, and I lived most of my life in the country," Bowman said. "So being a Black kid in the sixties over in Athens, I was pretty naive. When I came up here to Baylor, I was somewhat skeptical because I'd never been around a bunch of guys from big schools, big cities. So I was somewhat uncomfortable. I wasn't sure of my abilities to play with those guys from Houston, Dallas, different cities in California. Larry Gatewood was an All-American high school player from Oklahoma City. I was just concerned if I was going to be able to compete."

Sibley and Croucher were walk-ons, but they weren't intimidated about getting in games and mixing it up at Marrs McLean. Sibley described the "stratification" that often occurs in pick-up games and which took place as the Baylor players got together and played in the early fall of 1966. He said Bowman was the only Black player on the court, but that didn't make much difference in either a positive or negative way. The group came together, and they knew that some of the walk-ons were better than some of the scholarship players, at least in the freshman class.

Bowman began to see that he could compete, that he did belong with the other Baylor players. There would be plenty of highs and lows in the weeks and years ahead, but the kid from Athens was a college basketball player, as were Sibley and Croucher. All of them would have an impact on the Bears' freshman team.

"I never got to the point where I was cocky or arrogant or anything like that, but I finally got to the point where no matter where I played or who I played with, I could hold my own," Bowman said.

Oddly, though, Bowman looks back and believes Dawson failed to deliver on one of his recruiting promises. "I think the last time I talked to Carroll I said, 'Carroll, you never did talk to me about those weaknesses.'"

The 1966–67 Baylor Cubs team picture, including (top row, l.-r.) Sam Weaver, Tommy Bowman, Larry Gatewood, Clay Woods, David Sibley, Owen Fuller, Robert Waddell, (bottom row, l.-r.) Danny Elam, David Croucher, (coach) Carroll Dawson, David Fisher, and Ernie Armstrong.

Courtesy of Baylor Athletics via the Bowman Family

3
Freshman Season
Fall of 1966

One of the perceived strengths of sports is objectivity. Two teams meet on the field or court, and the more talented, more experienced, better prepared side wins the day. Popularity and rhetoric don't enter the equation.

But even if that's true on the playing field, the world of sports is still overflowing with subjectivity, spin, and hyperbole. Hype was a part of sports media long before Grantland Rice learned to read. Because all sportswriters are also sports fans, they can't help but put their enthusiasm into their copy. That's how ordinary eighteen-year-olds become superheroes overnight. Every student athlete who walks onto a college campus has the potential to be the next big thing. It's glaringly obvious in 2022, but it was just as true in 1966.

Tommy Bowman doesn't recall being a heavily recruited high school basketball player. His freshman team coach at Baylor, Carroll Dawson, said the first time he heard of Bowman was from a service station attendant, and, at that moment, the coach had no recruiting material to support the claim.

James Cash remembers his college coach, TCU's Buster Brannon, telling him that Bowman was a star recruit prior to the Athens High School senior's visit to Fort Worth.

Maybe the truth is somewhere in between. Either way, when Bowman prepared to suit up in a Baylor uniform for the Cubs freshman team on December 2, 1966, *Waco News-Tribune* staffer Jim Montgomery put the narrative in print: "Cub coach Carroll Dawson nominated a starting lineup which will have 6–8 Clay Wood of Plainview, 6–5 David Sibley of Houston Jones, 6–5 Larry Gatewood of Oklahoma City Classen, 6–4 Tommy Bowman of Athens, and 5–10 David Croucher of Houston Austin. . . . Bowman, widely sought as a schoolboy, is Baylor's first Negro cager [basketball player]."

Considering Dawson's excitement about having signed Bowman, his easy friendship with sportswriters through the decades, and the way sports journalism worked in those days, it's likely Dawson himself informed Montgomery about Bowman, who along with Gatewood gave Baylor a pair of star freshmen.

For his part, Bowman was still a little bit amazed to even be playing basketball at the Southwest Conference school. And yet, he didn't let that stop him from competing for and earning a starting spot.

The Baylor basketball players officially came together when practice began on October 15. By that time, Bowman, Sibley, and Croucher, who met on day one at Marrs McLean Gym, had sized up the talent in the program, figuring out each other's strengths and weaknesses for the better part of two months of pick-up games. Apparently, Dawson recognized a lot of the same attributes in his freshmen charges, since the walk-ons Sibley and Croucher were inserted into the starting lineup for the season opener.

Bowman, right on cue, made an immediate impact for the Cubs as he scored a team-high twenty-four points and pulled in fourteen rebounds, leading Baylor to an 86–60 victory over Navarro Junior College in the season-opening contest. That's a big-time double-double in modern basketball parlance, though Bowman doesn't remember anyone talking about double-doubles back then and he certainly wasn't tracking them (Bowman averaged 13.4 points and 9.6 rebounds during his three varsity seasons at Baylor; in his best statistical season he scored 15.3 points and grabbed 10.9 rebounds per game to average a double-double as a junior).

Basketball was kind of a tool for survival for Bowman. It allowed him to make friends through competition on the court. Those buddies formed a security blanket around him as he walked through a world in which he was both a pioneer and potential target for those resisting social change.

"I was surprised at how well things went when I was at Baylor," Bowman said. "There was turmoil everywhere in the country, and I kind of expected to deal with the same kinds of issues. But I never did. I don't think it was because I was such a terrific guy, a terrific personality. I kind of hung with the basketball players. I didn't go all over campus. I stayed with guys that could protect me, and they looked after me. I'm a country kid from Athens. That was the first time I'd ever been away from home. God just blessed me."

While he was bonding with his basketball teammates and excelling as the Baylor basketball program's first African American player, the part of life that took place away from the basketball court wasn't as comfortable.

⋇　⋇　⋇

The fall of 1966 was a heck of a time to be alive for a white college freshman starting school at Baylor. The front end of the Baby Boomers generation was coming into its own just as The Beatles were in the midst of reinventing rock music, having just released *Revolver* and toured the United States that summer. The Dallas Cowboys were on the rise with Don Meredith playing quarterback and the venerable Tom Landry running the show as head coach. The Baylor football team played in one of the top football conferences in the country, though the Bears were in the beginning stages of an eleven-year bowl drought. The Vietnam War was a low rumble, but the draft lottery was still years in the future.

College students in Waco could live among their kind in the almost completely self-sufficient "Baylor Bubble." Sure, there were dress codes and curfews—more stringent for women than men—and students technically weren't allowed to dance, or at least the Baptist school didn't sanction dance functions. But there were relaxing good times to be had shooting pool and playing pinball right across Dutton Avenue from the dorms at the Golden Q. George's, a long-famous bar and grill just across the highway from campus, was in its infancy but on the radar of the college crowd.

There were hippies, and there were rednecks. There was turmoil around the country, but Baylor was mostly insulated from the scandals, riots, and violence. Bowman's white teammates and friends, guys like Croucher and Sibley and classmate Woody Rogers, just shrug and search their memories for anything that resembled the turbulent sixties during their Baylor experience. Only looking back do they realize it must have been difficult for Bowman.

It was one thing for Bowman to get on the basketball court and let his skill, athleticism, and hard-earned confidence do the talking. It was another to walk into a classroom where he would have been one of very few Black students.

"I'll tell you, I was uncomfortable," Bowman said. "Whenever they called on me to say something, make comments, or ask me a question or something, I was very uncomfortable, to tell you the truth. I was reluctant to ask questions because I thought, 'I'm probably the only one in here that doesn't know the answer to the question.' So rather than me asking a question and sounding dumb, I just sat there. It took me awhile to realize that there are no dumb questions. It took me awhile. It took me a long while, like two or three years before I was comfortable making a comment or answering a question. I just didn't have that self-confidence."

Flipping through the 1967 Baylor yearbook reveals pages and pages of white students in the freshman class. Bowman isn't pictured, but neither are his basketball teammates among the individual headshots. His roommate, Tommy Reaux, is one of the few Black students represented. Baylor's first Black students were able to enroll for the 1964–65 school year and made up a tiny percentage of the student body throughout the college lives of Bowman and Reaux.

Although Bowman took a long time to adjust and feel comfortable participating in class, that doesn't mean he was actually falling behind in his academic pursuits. As a student in the business school, Bowman took many classes that required engagement to succeed, and he eventually got there. Public speaking presented an especially alarming prospect, as it does for most people regardless of race, gender, or where they grew up.

Dr. George M. Stokes, a speech communication professor who would become known as the "Voice of Baylor," had Bowman in a course that required making speeches in front of the class. He didn't let Bowman off the hook. Even six decades later, Bowman recalls the fear that overtook him. To get through it, he stared at the doorway, never looking at his fellow students and certainly not making eye contact.

Dr. Stokes sympathized with the unique challenge his class put in front of Bowman and took time to offer encouragement. The professor likely understood the kind of dividends it could pay after college. During his time working as an executive for Central Freight, Bowman excelled at giving speeches and became known for his clarity and humor as a speaker.

"It's hard to advance in the professional world if you can't stand up and make a presentation," Bowman said. "Looking back on it, Dr. Stokes, I think he recognized the issue that I was dealing with. There were so few Blacks at Baylor at the time, any class that you were in, you were going to be the only one that was in there. Dr. Stokes did a lot of things for me and said a lot of things to me, and I know he did it just to make me feel comfortable."

Only in retrospect does Bowman see those victories in the classroom. In the moment, it was a constant challenge to separate from his teammates and walk into classes where he stood out. For white students, having a Black classmate might not have been a distraction. None of Bowman's teammates or white friends remember specific cases when they were in an integrated environment in their academic work.

The one clue that the Baylor basketball players were given into Bowman's internal struggle came from the way he played in practice. There were days when the freshman from Athens walked onto the court with a different kind of aggression.

Early in their structured workouts, Sibley noticed one day when Bowman was oddly inclined toward hard fouling during a fast break drill. It was a three-on-two live action sequence, and Bowman was on the shorthanded defensive unit. When Croucher went into the lane, Bowman took him out. When it was Sibley's turn, Bowman did the same.

Sibley didn't give him a pass.

"I faked and did something, and he gave me a big shove," Sibley said. "I had the basketball. I turned around and threw a two-handed pass right off his chest and I went for him."

Sibley said fights in the gym were part of the scene. If two guys started fighting, it was such a commonplace occurrence that the other guys waiting it out might just take a water break until the fight resolved itself. So, when he went for Bowman, he intended for it to be a rumble.

"I'm going at Tommy. They jumped in real quick," Sibley said. "It's the first Black scholarship player at Baylor, and this white walk-on is going at him and I want to get him."

The incident ignited something between the two freshmen. Not a bitter rivalry but a sense of mutual respect grew from there. Bowman and Sibley would eventually be roommates at Baylor and remained lifelong friends. Bowman said he regards Sibley as his closest friend.

"I kind of remember we were really good friends after that," Sibley said. "Before, we got along fine, and playing with a Black player wasn't any big deal. But I felt like we were friends after that. We would hang out together after that."

✦   ✦   ✦

Unlike today's college basketball world where heralded freshmen make their debut on the varsity squad at the start of November (freshmen teams are a thing of the past), Bowman, Sibley, and their classmates had a slower transition into student-athlete life. Practice began in mid-October and lasted six weeks. Because the season started on December 2, much of the nonconference slate took place in mid-to-late December when the rest of campus emptied out for

Christmas break. That was a bonding time for the entire program. Russell Kibbe, who was a fifth-year senior for Baylor in 1967–68 when Bowman eventually played on the Bears' varsity as a sophomore, recalls those days when the team had the dorm to themselves. He recalls Bowman playing cards and fitting in as just one of the guys.

After the win over Navarro College to start the season, Baylor played Temple Junior College four days later. While Bowman scored in double figures again with eleven, that night proved to be a break-out game for Larry Gatewood. The tall, versatile, offensive-minded guard from Oklahoma City had been a heralded recruit but was also a Baylor legacy as the son of former football standout Lester "Buddy" Gatewood. Buddy Gatewood was a center for the Bears football team and was drafted by the Green Bay Packers in 1943. Larry Gatewood, at the time of this writing, still ranks twenty-fifth on the career scoring list for Baylor basketball despite playing just three varsity seasons. He scored thirty-seven to lead the Baylor freshmen past Temple in the Cubs' second game together.

Meanwhile, Dawson was navigating a new season with added responsibility. The Cubs would play a double-round-robin schedule against SWC opponents Texas, Texas A&M, TCU, and SMU in January and February. That portion of the schedule would present its own challenges as Bowman was the only African American freshman in the conference at that point. During December, though, Baylor would travel to some games in smaller cities to play junior college squads.

Dawson was on the lookout.

"It's hard to explain how the culture was in those days," Dawson said. "It was murder. There were fights all the time, people getting run out of restaurants. It was bad.

"I'd go into a McDonald's and get all sack lunches, and we'd go to some park and eat. I never went into a restaurant. A couple years later, (Bowman) said, 'I realize now you were trying to keep me from getting hung, weren't you?'"

Bowman doesn't recall any scary scenes at junior college gyms. He doesn't even remember eating burgers on park benches. He viewed his place on the team and his teammates themselves as a protective cocoon. Although he was aware of the kind of violent scenes unfolding throughout the country at the time and knew it could happen around him at some point, he said it never did. There would be at least one brawl on the court during Bowman's career, but it revolved around competitive rivalry and machismo taking the place of common sense.

As he bonded with his teammates, Bowman quickly understood his place within Baylor's on-court strategy. He had a combination of size, quickness, and vertical leap that allowed him to guard just about anybody. Therefore, it became his job to defend the opponent's best offensive player on most nights. Once he figured out he could do that, he gained a greater belief in his overall place on the team.

"I think confidence is essential to do anything, whether it be athletics or academics or business," Bowman said. "I think you've got to be comfortable within yourself that you can do whatever it is you need to be doing."

Pretty soon, Bowman was relaxed enough to give the business back to his combustible freshman coach.

While Dawson constantly stayed on guard, making sure Bowman was in safe situations, especially on the road, it didn't diminish the coach's competitive spirit. One night during nonconference play, Baylor didn't live up to expectations at Hill Junior College in Hillsboro, Texas, just up the road from Waco.

Sibley said Hill's coach was a friend of Dawson's, so that probably made matters worse when the junior college team beat the Cubs, 87–77. The team filed back on the bus, well aware that their coach was steaming.

"Dawson is the last one on the bus. He sits up at the front, doesn't acknowledge anybody on the bus," Sibley said. "So we're afraid for the thirty-five-minute drive back home. When the bus pulls up at Baylor, he doesn't say anything to us except 'practice tomorrow.'"

Dawson's anger over the December setback against Hill Junior College hadn't eased at all by the time practice began the next day. He was likely looking for one error in the workout that would allow him to vent his frustration through good old-fashioned punitive sprinting. Like millions of basketball players since then, the Cubs knew the pain of "horses," sometimes called "lines" or even "suicides." It's the practice of sprinting from the baseline to the free-throw line and back, then the baseline to half court and back, then the baseline to the opposite free-throw line and back, then baseline to baseline and back. Sibley said they sprinted for so long that it felt like a death march.

"Somewhere in there, Dawson says something like, 'This is hurting me more than it's hurting you,'" Sibley said. "Bowman says, 'Coach, I'm sorry to hear that because I know how bad this must be hurting you.' Dawson laughed. It's kind of like it broke the spell. All the sudden he said that was enough."

Carroll Dawson.

Courtesy of Baylor Athletics via the Texas Collection

4
Carroll Dawson

The time had come for Carroll Dawson to make a decision.

After working his way through a box of VHS tapes of the world's greatest women's basketball players, the first call was the easy one. Dawson and the Houston Comets wanted Sheryl Swoopes. This was the initial WNBA player allotment, a process guided at least partially by geography, and Swoopes was a regional draw because she had led Texas Tech to a national championship four years earlier. Oh and by the way, she was also considered to be one of the best—if not *the* best—women's basketball players in the world at that moment.

But Dawson still had a pick to make as the WNBA divvied out the ranks of international basketball players to populate the rosters of North America's newest and biggest swing so far at a pro women's hoops league.

The problem for the Houston Rockets general manager, who had been tasked with running the Houston Comets as well, was that he'd never actually met the player whose name he wanted to call. As the day drew near, he couldn't make contact with her because she was apparently skiing with her boyfriend in the Italian Alps, one of the perks of playing in the Italian women's league.

Dawson threw caution to the wind, put his hand down on the table and said, "Cynthia Cooper."

"I immediately had a sick feeling in my stomach," Dawson said.

That uneasiness in his gut, buyer's remorse he called it, stayed with him for a few days. Then he bumped into an old, reliable friend. Robert Reid spent seven seasons playing for the Houston Rockets when Dawson was an assistant coach for Del Harris and then Bill Fitch. Reid came off the bench to average double digits in scoring for Houston teams that made the NBA Finals in 1981 and 1986. Reid and Dawson had been to war together many times on the brightest stages of pro basketball.

Reid congratulated Dawson on the selection of Cooper for the Comets. The Rockets and Comets executive didn't know it, but Cooper was a Houston resident who played pick-up basketball at the gym where Reid and many other high-profile hoopsters hung out. In fact, Reid said, she was the only non-Rocket they let play.

Dawson was relieved. If he could've seen the future on that winter's day in 1997, he would've been considerably more upbeat.

Cooper, now a Naismith Hall of Famer, earned WNBA MVP honors in 1997 and 1998. She played a leading role, scoring more than twenty-one points and dishing out almost five assists per game as the Comets won the first four WNBA championships.

It was a good pick. But what possessed Dawson to pull the trigger and go against his personal rules for player evaluation? Was it the same voice that led him to drive down a country road in Athens, Texas, on the chance that Tommy Bowman really was the best basketball player in the state of Texas? Maybe, although more than thirty years separated those two moments. But where did that voice come from? It's more than a little bit likely that Dawson's instinct developed as a result of him once being a nobody from nowhere.

Dawson grew up in the 1950s playing hoops with white and Black kids in school gyms and on outdoor, makeshift courts in tiny Alba, Texas and surrounding towns. Alba was mostly white, partly because it was so small that there weren't enough jobs for Black people to make a living in the community, according to Dawson. But since it was a farming town, people would come through at certain times of the year when there was seasonal work. "I had a lot of friends that were Black that I played with when I would go down to my aunt's [close to Kilgore]," he said. "The Black people would come in during the fall and pick cotton. I always got along. There was no problem there."

Dawson was so enthralled with the game of basketball that he would hitchhike as a high school kid to watch his favorite team, the Tyler Junior College Apaches. In doing so, he developed a relationship with Apaches coach Floyd Wagstaff. As a senior at Alba High School, he was all set to sign with Tyler.

Until, of all things, an arm-wrestling competition at a county fair altered his course. Ever the competitor, Dawson couldn't resist the arm-wrestling booth while enjoying a day at the Old Settlers Reunion in Quitman, Texas. The day before he was supposed to sign with Tyler, he arm wrestled all day until he strained a tendon in his right arm. When he arrived at Tyler Junior College, Wagstaff was away on an excursion to either buy or sell a horse. The assistant coach in charge lumped Dawson in with sixty other potential signees, all trying out for a few spots. Limited to going left, a skill he had never developed to that point, Dawson was one of the first ten players cut.

"After three years of going to every game that I could, I go back home and I'm almost in tears," Dawson said. "My dad asked what was the matter. I said, 'I got cut.' He said, 'You got cut? That coach has been living with us.'"

Nonetheless, Carroll's father, Julie Dawson, heard of a potential fallback. Paris Junior College phoned the house while Carroll had been in Tyler underwhelming the Apaches' assistant coach. Instead of calling Wagstaff to plead his case (text messaging was still more than forty years in the future), Dawson returned Paris's call and signed with them instead of Tyler. He said Wagstaff refused to speak to him for the next twenty years. But the circumstances worked out for Paris JC. Dawson became a junior college All-American at the school and caught the attention of the major college basketball world. He had more than fifty scholarship offers by the time his sophomore season at Paris was in full swing.

Once again, though, Dawson's path took a sharp turn away from its logical destination. In the spring of 1958, he picked the University of Kansas as his next school because he wanted to play with superstar Wilt Chamberlain. However, when he arrived in Lawrence, Kansas at the beginning of August he learned that the Jayhawks' big man had flown the coop to play for the Harlem Globetrotters.

So much for that.

Dawson returned to Texas and decided to give Baylor a try. A relative drove him to Waco, where he sat down with Bill Henderson, who guided the Bears to the NCAA title game in 1948 and remained as Baylor's coach until 1961.

"This is sometimes how you've got an angel on your shoulder," said Dawson, who described his first encounter with Tommy Bowman's mother in a similar way. "I get down there, and Mr. Bill Henderson is the coach and Bill Menefee is the assistant. [Henderson] meets me at the back of Martin Hall on those steps. We're sitting there with my uncle. [Henderson] said, 'I've looked everywhere. I've got no scholarships. I don't see how I can get you here.' So I said, 'Well, ok. I'll go try SMU.' School had started two weeks before. I got up, and I started to the car. I had my hand on the door. Mr. Bill said, 'Hold on, I've got one idea.' He runs up the stairs to the phone. He comes back and says, 'Ok, Jack Patterson, the track coach, has a scholarship, and he's going to loan it to me until mid-term, and I'll have a scholarship for you, so you're here.' I was within one step of not going to Baylor."

+   +   +

Dawson might have become the architect of a powerhouse Baylor basketball program long before Kim Mulkey or Scott Drew had the chance to do so. For better or worse, however, the Heart O' Texas Coliseum stopped that from happening.

In its time, the HOT Coliseum served a purpose in that it gave the basketball team a place to play. It didn't have permanent locker rooms, and the structure of the seats was more suited to indoor rodeo than basketball. But in the mid-twentieth century, football got the glory and basketball got the right to exist.

While the Bears' program has ascended to national prominence and an almost unfathomable dominating run to a national championship in 2021, it definitely wasn't always that way. In fact, between one rise and the next there was a gap of more than fifty years.

Henderson guided Baylor to the national championship game in 1948 and the national semifinals in 1950. But between that "Final Four" appearance in 1950 and Drew's first NCAA Tournament qualifier at Baylor in 2008, the Bears made just one NCAA Tournament (1988).* When Baylor made the national championship game in 1948 and the national semifinals in 1950, the semifinalists didn't even all gather at the same venue. The West final was the national semifinal, and the winner went on to the championship game in New York.

In the meantime, Baylor men's basketball made the news more often with scandals within the program, including an academic transgression in the 1990s and a horrendous series of events in which a Baylor player named Carlton Dotson murdered teammate Patrick Dennehy in 2003.

Through the 1950s, 1960s, and 1970s, the NCAA Tournament was not the reward for an above average season that it has become in the twenty-first century. It blossomed in both size and popularity in the 1980s. When Dawson played at Baylor, and even through the time when he served as the Bears' head coach from 1973 to 1977, it wasn't the Big Dance. In 1977, the first year of the "Final Four" designation, the NCAA Tournament had a thirty-two-team field, and only SWC champ Arkansas made it.

Dawson earned All-Conference honors as a senior in 1960 as he helped Baylor finish with a 12–12 record and take sixth in the SWC standings. During Bowman's three years on the Bears' varsity squad (1967–68 to 1969–70), they finished second twice and tied for third once, which represented the most sustained period of excellence for

*   Author's note: The NCAA didn't trademark the term "Final Four" until 1977.

Baylor basketball in the fifty-plus–year period between 1950 and 2008.

For many of those years, Baylor played in the all-purpose, barn-like HOT Coliseum. (The arena, located more than five miles from the Baylor campus, is still in use as of this writing. Its name has been changed to the Extraco Events Center.) Baylor opened the on-campus Ferrell Center in 1988, and it eventually saw the Lady Bears ascend to the top of their game with a national championship in 2005. Scott Drew took over Baylor's men's program in 2003 in the aftermath of the Dotson scandal and built it from the ground up. Drew's Bears made the NCAA Tournament in 2008, followed it with an appearance in the National Invitation Tournament finals in 2009, and then advanced to the NCAA Elite Eight in 2010 before losing to eventual champion Duke.

✦   ✦   ✦

After his playing career ended, Dawson jumped at the chance to serve as Menefee's assistant coach when Menefee took over for Henderson in 1961. Dawson coached Baylor's Cubs freshman team through the 1972–73 season and then took over for Menefee as Baylor's head coach before the 1973–74 campaign. Dawson led Baylor until 1977. But, among other factors, he determined he couldn't overcome the dead weight of the Bears' home arena.

"It killed our recruiting," Dawson said. "It was used against us so bad. Recruiting to (the HOT Coliseum) when you didn't have a place to play was really tough at the time. I quit. I went to work with the Dallas Cowboys. We weren't supported by the number of people that they are now. In the 60s we all lived off football."

Ultimately, though, Dawson was a basketball visionary. As a Baylor assistant, he could see how college basketball was moving. Not only had Texas Western won the national title with an all-Black starting five, the University of Houston, not yet a member of the SWC, integrated in 1964 when Guy Lewis signed Elvin Hayes and Don Chaney. Lewis's Cougars would go on to host the "Game of the

Century" in the Astrodome when John Wooden's UCLA Bruins came to town in 1968.

"There were 55,000 people there," recalled Dawson, who watched the game on prime-time television. "The next day in the paper I said basketball is going to be the next revenue sport in college. I was laughed out of town. But I got the last laugh."

After two years working for Cowboys' team president Tex Schramm, a period when the otherwise lifelong basketball man would shrewdly absorb the inner workings of a successful pro sports franchise, Dawson went back to the basketball court.

He found a home with the Houston Rockets and remained with the organization for most of the next three decades. Dawson's time in Houston as an assistant coach under Harris, Fitch, Chaney, and Rudy Tomjanovich coincides with the franchise's glory years. He was on the bench for all four of the Rockets' Western Conference titles and their two World Championships in 1994 and 1995.

When Dawson arrived in Houston, the roster included Moses Malone, Reid, Tomjanovich, Calvin Murphy, and Mike Dunleavy. That team defeated the Kansas City Kings in the West finals and then lost in six games against the Boston Celtics in the NBA Finals.

In 1983, Houston won the NBA draft lottery and selected seven-foot-four center Ralph Sampson with the first overall pick. The Rockets hit the jackpot again in 1984, allowing them to pick Hakeem Olajuwon and complete the famed "Twin Towers." With those two playing a central role, Houston knocked off the "Showtime" Los Angeles Lakers in the 1986 Western Conference finals. But once again they were beaten by the Celtics in six games of the NBA Finals. That would be the height of Sampson's NBA life. However, Olajuwon remained the centerpiece of the team through the end of the twentieth century, leading the Rockets to the promised land along with Tomjanovich, Kenny Smith, Otis Thorpe, Robert Horry, Vernon Maxwell, and, of course, Dawson.

After moving to the general manager's office in 1996, Dawson played a central role in acquiring seven-foot-six Chinese phenom Yao Ming in 2002 and American superstar Tracy McGrady in 2004.

Oh and by the way, he also assembled the greatest women's basketball team in history, with the possible exception of various gold-medal-winning Team USA squads. Led by Cooper, Swoopes, and Tina Thompson on the court and coached by Van Chancellor, the Houston Comets went 71–19 on the way to the first three WNBA titles.

Dawson's hunch, it's safe to say, paid off.

Carroll Dawson coaching.

Courtesy of Baylor Athletics via the Texas Collection

5
Freshman Season
SWC Play, 1967

Carroll Dawson and the Baylor freshman basketball team had way too much time to think about their loss to Hill College, which closed the early portion of their season on December 14. After Dawson drove his point home with a long and brutal cardio session on December 15, the Cubs had a break from live competition. It would be more than six weeks before they got on the court against anyone but themselves and the Bears varsity team.

At the start of 1967, freshman eligibility was on the distant horizon. A *New York Times* article from January 9, 1972 reported that the NCAA took a vote and easily passed basketball freshman eligibility during its annual convention held in Hollywood, Florida. The vote for freshmen football players to be allowed to play varsity was closer, 94–67, with small colleges abstaining as they already deployed freshmen. The *Times* story noted that the move took Penn State's Joe Paterno by surprise, and he had not yet decided whether or not to abolish his freshman football team. Meanwhile, Rutgers football coach John Batemen expressed his belief that a team that needed freshmen in the lineup must not be very good.

As 1967 began, Tommy Bowman and his teammates were expected to adapt to the rigors of college academics. Part of the reason for the long break between games was for the freshmen to concentrate on their end-of-semester exams, which took place in

January when students came back from their holiday break. The freshmen also played a role in helping the varsity prepare for the upcoming conference schedule.

Baylor's varsity basketball team posted a record of 14–10, with eight wins and six losses in Southwest Conference action during the 1966–67 campaign. That was good enough to tie for second place as the rest of the SWC floundered in the wake of an SMU squad that won twenty games and went 12–2 in conference. It's impossible to know if the likes of Larry Gatewood, Bowman, and David Sibley could have helped Baylor close the gap behind the Mustangs. Ultimately, though, the SWC's tardiness in integrating its sports teams was put under the microscope during the 1967 NCAA Tournament. The stellar SMU team, which had trounced the rest of the conference, won its postseason opener against Louisville. But Houston, led by Elvin Hayes's thirty-one points and eleven rebounds and a complementary double-double by Don Chaney, defeated the Mustangs, 83–75, in the Midwest Region final for a berth in the national semifinals.

Basketball, still sometimes referred to as "cage" in the local sports section, took a back seat to football in the college sports hierarchy. That's the case in some quarters of the country even during the mid-twenty-first century. However, the Waco newspapers—the *Waco News Tribune* and *Waco Times Herald* (the publications used the same writers and would eventually merge into the *Waco Tribune-Herald*)— treated basketball as front-of-the-sports-section content, and game stories were filed on all the Cubs' games as well.

The Waco paper ran a headline celebrating Gatewood's stellar night as the Cubs got back in action on January 31: "Gatewood Hits 31 Points as Cubs Whip Texas Frosh." Described as a "6-5 gunner from Oklahoma City," the offensive-minded Gatewood made twelve of nineteen field goals and put in seven more points from the free-throw line. Bowman found himself in foul trouble early in the second half but still had a dozen points, same as Sibley. David Croucher, who like Sibley was proving himself as a walk-on, contributed seventeen points in Baylor's 88–74 win at the Heart O' Texas Coliseum.

Gatewood and Croucher kept it up four days later against Texas A&M in a much closer ball game back at the HOT Coliseum. Bowman, perhaps still looking for the right balance of defensive aggression, fouled out with ten points. But Gatewood poured in thirty-nine, and Croucher added sixteen to keep the Cubs in it. Gatewood completed a three-point play with around a minute left in regulation to tie the game at seventy-three, and it went to overtime knotted up there. In the extra period, a seldom used player named Danny Elam made one of two free throws with eleven seconds left. It was Elam's only tally, but it was enough to give Baylor an 83–82 victory.

At that point, the Cubs had spent three and a half months practicing together mixed with a smattering of games, and the win over the Aggie freshmen improved Baylor's record to 4–1. Although it wasn't the usual rhythm of competition that goes along with a sports season, the Cubs' time together had them playing well, as they showed in back-to-back road games.

Baylor went to Fort Worth to play TCU on February 7. The Horned Frogs varsity handed the Bears a seven-point defeat, but the Cubs claimed the freshman contest. Gatewood further established his role as a volume shooter, and an effective one at that. He made ten of eighteen shots from the field and tossed in nine free throws to lead Baylor with twenty-nine points. Bowman's ability to track down rebounds was coming to the forefront as he was credited with seventeen boards to go along with fifteen points, another stellar double-double. Baylor was efficient on the offensive end as Croucher joined Bowman with fifteen points, and Sibley scored fourteen to give the Cubs four players in double digits en route to an 81–63 victory.

Four days later, Baylor made another short road trip to Dallas for a freshman-varsity doubleheader. SMU's varsity sat atop the SWC standings and claimed a six-point victory over the Bears. The SMU freshmen, known as the Colts, hadn't won a game to that point in the season, but they managed to challenge the Cubs for a half.

Baylor took a 41–40 lead to the break, then hammered SMU in the second half for an 87–63 win. Once again, Gatewood tallied twenty-nine points. The *Waco News Tribune* account noted that

Bowman scored eighteen and pulled down "what seemed like a zillion rebounds." Sibley had one of his best offensive games to date with twenty points.

In just two weeks, the Baylor freshmen had made one pass through their SWC schedule. The Cubs played an abbreviated conference slate against only Texas, Texas A&M, TCU, and SMU. Perhaps because they were longer trips, Baylor didn't play Texas Tech, Arkansas, or Rice in freshman games either at home or on the road. Even so, Baylor was the definite frontrunner in the smaller loop by mid-February.

The Cubs stayed on a roll on Valentine's Day of 1967 with a fourteen-point victory over TCU, earning Baylor the sweep of the Wogs, short for polliwogs (the newspaper especially tended to use diminutive nicknames for all of the SWC mascots). However, Dawson wasn't going to let his team's winning streak give them an inflated view of themselves. He told the *Waco News Tribune*, "We weren't too smooth. We got to running a 'give and go.' We'd give them the ball and they'd go down and score." Bowman still did his thing, pitching in sixteen points and grabbing eight rebounds. Gatewood hit seven of sixteen from the floor and eleven free throws to total twenty-five points, and Sibley muscled his way to thirteen rebounds.

When Bowman and his teammates look back on their college careers, and on Bowman's skill set specifically, his defense stands out. Anyone who digs in with basketball knows that most games are won on the defensive end. Long scoring runs that define a game's momentum happen as the result of one team winning successive battles on defense while putting the ball in the hoop on offense. The even more electrifying moment of a fast break doesn't usually happen without a deflection or steal on defense that gets it going. Bowman had the right combination of size, speed, and (less tangibly) discipline to excel on defense.

"Not that I'm any true barometer, but if he didn't want me to get a shot off in practice, I didn't get a shot off," Croucher said. "He was that much bigger. That's a part of it. He was athletic and he could move. He was tenacious."

Bowman came up with perhaps his most significant contribution of the season when Baylor traveled to Austin to play Texas on February 18. Baylor's Robert Waddell made a free throw to put the Cubs in front, 81–80, with twenty-five seconds left in overtime. Texas ran the clock down below ten seconds, then guard Bill Wright found a lane to the basket and appeared to have an open layup that would give the Yearlings the win. But Bowman swooped in and blocked Wright's shot with less than three seconds left. Baylor's Ernie Armstrong gathered in the loose ball, and the Cubs headed back north to Waco with their perfect conference record intact.

The Baylor freshmen were 9–1 on the season at that point, with six wins and zero losses against SWC opponents. They were front-runners to win the freshman conference championship and had a foursome of stars who were primed to make an impact on the varsity in the near future.

All of that took a back seat to the challenge that faced them next. Baylor was set to play Texas A&M on February 21 in the Aggies' G. Rollie White Coliseum.

Texas A&M became both an integrated and coeducational campus in the mid-1960s. Women were allowed to officially enroll and fully participate in campus activities in 1963. The inclusion of African American students was more sporadic and started with schools in Texas A&M's system such as Arlington State (which became University of Texas at Arlington in 1965) and Prairie View A&M. By mid-1967, African American students had formed a campus organization at Texas A&M, and the school's athletic department had signed Black student athletes to track and field scholarships.

As far as Dawson was concerned, though, there was plenty of reason to worry about taking Bowman into the hostile environment of Texas A&M's gym.

"I brought him up to my office. It was going really good. He was playing well, and we hadn't lost," Dawson said. "I brought him in and said, 'Look, now, I've been able to control the atmosphere so far, but this is going to be different. This is going to put a lot of pressure on you. They're going to try everything in the world to get you distracted.

They're going to call you everything in the world. All they want you to do is just react.' I said, 'Ignore them. Don't even look at them. Don't even acknowledge them and they'll finally quit.'"

Part of the intimidation of playing at G. Rollie White included the walk down a ramp from the dressing room on an upper level through the stands to the court. As the Baylor players descended into the Aggie crowd, one of those surreal events transpired that burned itself into the memories of Sibley and Bowman, who were walking side by side.

"They had little kids there. It's the same almost everywhere. Little kids, younger than ten," Sibley said. "There was this sweet little girl, just eight or nine. She's going, 'Fuck you, nigger!'"

In Sibley's memory, he and Bowman were startled but not rocked. They laughed it off. Bowman said he wasn't scarred by the experience.

"From a constitution standpoint, I'd gotten to be pretty comfortable with who I was. I wasn't easily set back," Bowman said. "A deal like that, you don't expect to see some cute little girl. You don't expect that. You expect that to come from a big, ugly guy in the stands. And it did."

Baylor survived the day without further incident, or at least anything that made the newspaper article. But Texas A&M won the game, 75–66. The Fish almost doubled up the Cubs in the rebounding category, and they clamped down on the prolific-scoring Gatewood, holding him to eleven points. Sibley led Baylor with twenty, and Bowman and Croucher added fifteen and thirteen, respectively.

Bowman said the racial invectives from the stands were louder and rougher at Texas A&M than any other place where Baylor played during his career. Dawson remembered the Cubs' game at Texas A&M as a contest that Baylor won. Perhaps that's how it felt to get away from there in one piece without any kind of a race riot.

"I called him up to the front [of the bus], and I said, 'Great job, just like I told you,'" Dawson recalled. "He said, 'Well, almost.' I said, 'What do you mean?' He said, 'Well you said eventually they'd quit. They never quit.'"

When the Cubs arrived back in Waco, they had a 9–2 record and one game left on the schedule. The Baylor freshmen hosted SMU on Friday afternoon, February 24 at Marrs McLean Gym. It was one of the few times the Baylor freshmen played a game separately from the varsity. But the Bears had faced the Mustangs on January 3, when the freshmen were still on break, so the Cubs and Colts finished up the season on Baylor's campus at the older gymnasium.

Despite the loss to Hill College in December that had so irked Dawson, and the recent setback at Texas A&M, the Cubs had proven their mettle over the course of three months and twelve games. They finished in style by pounding SMU, 79–62, in a contest that showcased many of the team's strengths.

Bowman scored twelve points and pulled in twenty-two rebounds. The *Waco News Tribune* game story noted that Baylor began to take over the game midway through the first half when Bowman and Gatewood started connecting on the offensive end. Gatewood scored twenty-two points before halftime, and the Cubs took a 35–26 advantage to intermission. The prolific scorer from Oklahoma City ended with thirty-six in the season finale as he made fourteen of twenty-three shots from the field and added eight made free throws. Sibley scored nine and hit double digits in rebounds with eleven. Although Croucher scored in double figures in six SWC games, he only had five versus the Colts.

By taking care of business against SMU, Baylor's freshmen posted a 10–2 record, which was the program's best "in modern memory" according to the *Waco News Tribune*. The newspaper report noted that the Cubs' mark surpassed that of the 1952 team that went 9–3. Not bad for a squad that only had a couple of scholarship players as key contributors. Sibley and Croucher spent their high school years competing in the big city, both for their high school teams and in ultra-intense pick-up games in the summer. They figured they had the skill to walk-on for Baylor, and they backed it up on the court as they helped elevate the team. They weren't blown away by the talent they faced upon arriving in Waco and therefore didn't have high expectations.

"I didn't think we were that good," Sibley said. "We ended up winning the conference championship for freshmen."

Bowman was thriving on the basketball court. He averaged 15.6 points during 1966–67 as a complementary scorer to Gatewood, who hit for twenty-six per game. The newspaper accounts gave rebounding totals for a few of the freshman contests. Not counting the vagueness of the report that Bowman grabbed "what seemed like a zillion" boards versus SMU in Dallas, the freshman from Athens averaged more than fifteen rebounds. His tenacity on the defensive end, including the key block against Texas in Austin, was often cited as well.

Along with Bowman's trackable statistics during games, he had found a place among teammates and friends. As the first Black scholarship athlete at Baylor, like in so many stories about being the first Black anything in the American sports world of the mid-twentieth century, survival was the foremost goal.

"I can remember we would warm up and sometimes a ball would get away and roll toward the stands," Bowman said. "I would jog over there and get the ball, and one guy would start saying, 'You bring your such and such over here if you want to.' I just turned around and got back on the court. That's where I felt safe."

Dawson admitted that he was in some ways dreading going through a season with the school's first African American student athlete. He was amazed, looking back, on how smoothly it actually turned out, though he remained on edge throughout the experience.

The former coach credited an angel on his shoulder that led him to recruit Bowman. With the benefit of hindsight, Dawson can see that the proverbial divine intervention played out both on the basketball court and the way Bowman adapted to life at Baylor.

"[Bowman] just grew up," Dawson said. "He did everything the right way. It's hard to explain how anybody that young was so mature about it. That was not the easiest thing to do, what he did. I can't explain how bad it was. There were fights, race riots, all kinds of things going on. You'd have never known at Baylor. I've got to give more than Tommy credit. I've got to give our other players credit and the student body."

6
The Summer of Love

After Guy V. Lewis's Houston team defeated SWC champ SMU in the Midwest Region final of the 1967 NCAA Tournament in Lawrence, Kansas, the Cougars advanced to play UCLA in the national semifinals. But Houston wasn't yet up to the challenge the Bruins presented.

UCLA's Lew Alcindor, who converted to Islam in 1968 and changed his name to Kareem Abdul-Jabbar, totaled nineteen points and twenty rebounds to lead his team to a fifteen-point win over Houston at Freedom Hall in Louisville, Kentucky. The next night, Alcindor had a similar double-double, and UCLA stomped Dayton by fifteen for the national championship. That marked the first of the Bruins' seven consecutive national championships.

John Wooden ultimately led UCLA to ten NCAA Tournament titles between 1964 and 1975.

Elsewhere in California, the counterculture was making moves. The Grateful Dead, rising out of the Haight-Ashbury neighborhood of San Francisco, played the Human Be In and the Mantra-Rock Dance in January of 1967. The Dead, along with the Jimi Hendrix Experience and The Mamas & the Papas, closed out the Monterey Pop Festival on June 18, 1967. The Summer of Love was off and running.

But violent race riots also plagued that summer. In Detroit, civilians, many of them African Americans, clashed with police over the course of five days in late July. More than a thousand buildings were burned, and forty-three people died. The Detroit riot closely followed a similar uprising in Newark, New Jersey, in mid-July that killed twenty-six. Other such incidents erupted in Los Angeles, Harlem, Chicago, Minneapolis, and Birmingham.

Tommy Bowman stayed away from all of it. He even stayed away from the basketball court for the most part during that summer. He went home to Athens and worked at a brickyard from seven in the morning until midafternoon. By the time he finished a hard day of physical labor, he was too tired to do much else. There really weren't many places to play basketball, anyway, save for his friends' backyard hoops around the neighborhood.

It was uneventful, perhaps for the best. The heavy lifting at the brickyard kept him in shape and motivated to get back to his teammates for the fall semester.

Baylor forward Tommy Bowman (25) jumps to block a shot as TCU
forward James Cash (54) looks on.

Courtesy of Baylor Athletics via the Texas Collection

7
Sophomore Season
Fall of 1967

As the 1967–68 season began, media attention on the Baylor basketball team focused on the availability of six-foot-five senior forward Ed Thorpe, who had suffered a knee injury in the offseason. The potential for Tommy Bowman, Larry Gatewood, and David Sibley to make an impact on the Baylor varsity began as a secondary plot.

Gatewood, although he didn't start the season opener and came off the bench for most of the year, changed the narrative in the Bears' first game. He led Baylor with twenty-two points as the Bears began with a 90–61 victory over Austin College.

Bowman debuted on the varsity with nine points and four rebounds, though his effort might have been too subtle for most observers. Jim Montgomery's *Waco Tribune-Herald* game report didn't mention Bowman by name, although it did emphasize that the Bears, as a team, held Austin College to thirteen made field goals. Baylor coach Bill Menefee used twelve players in the lopsided win, and eleven of them scored points. Bowman was the third leading scorer behind Gatewood and Sibley, who finished with twelve. But Sibley's points came on ten field goal attempts, while Bowman went three for four from the field. The newspaper account didn't frame it as such, but all three sophomores outshined Thorpe, who had four points and one rebound. That theme would continue.

The newspaper account didn't single out Bowman as the first Black player to take the court for the Baylor varsity. Perhaps the readers of the *Tribune-Herald* were deemed sophisticated enough to have remembered that Bowman broke the barrier the year before as a freshman. It's more likely, though, that the sportswriter just scooted past the landmark. Although integration was altering the rosters at the high school and college level throughout the southern United States and Texas, even forward-thinking *Tribune-Herald* sports editor Dave Campbell made light mention of the phenomenon.

In Baylor's second game, Sibley's twenty-one points led the Bears to a 93–78 win over Centenary in Shreveport, Louisiana, and Bowman took his turn as top scorer with sixteen in an 80–70 loss at Louisiana Lafayette.

It wasn't until the fourth game of the campaign that Baylor showed signs of what it could do when its various pieces began to fit together. The Bears hosted Tulane, which ended the previous season with five straight wins and had started hot in the fall of 1967. Five Baylor players scored in double figures, led by Russell Kibbe's nineteen and seventeen apiece from Randy Thompson and Sibley. This time, Bowman's contributions were documented. The fifth paragraph of Montgomery's game report read: "Tommy Bowman belongs on the list, too. He scored only six points, but he blocked shots, tipped in two shots, and grabbed eight rebounds." In the next paragraph, Menefee was quoted pointing out that "Bowman had them thinking about those blocked shots."

Baylor lurched back and forth through its nonconference schedule in December of 1967. The win over Tulane ignited a three-game winning streak for Baylor at the Heart O' Texas Coliseum. Bowman had a double-double, his first on the varsity, as he posted sixteen points and twelve rebounds in a victory over Loyola of New Orleans. Sibley led the Bears with twenty-two points in that game as he crept closer and closer to earning a scholarship.

On December 19, Bowman led Baylor in scoring with seventeen points as the Bears rolled up a 92–74 win over Texas–Arlington. The easy win, in which the Bears starters gave way to reserves for long chunks of the contest, improved Baylor's record to five wins with just one loss.

If the young Bears team was starting to feel a little mojo, a correction followed. Oklahoma City came to town and dealt Baylor an eight-point defeat. The Chiefs were semi-regulars in the NCAA Tournament under coach Abe Lemons in those days as they made the national bracket seven times between 1955 and 1973. Larry Gatewood, playing against his hometown university, came off the bench and set a Baylor record by tossing in sixteen field goals on his way to thirty-three points. Bowman gathered in ten rebounds, but he couldn't find the range on the offensive end. Other than Gatewood, the rest of the Bears combined to make just sixteen of fifty shots and lost at home for the first time that season.

Baylor traveled to Alabama immediately after Christmas and took another loss at the hands of the Crimson Tide, 85–75, in the Mobile Cage Classic. The Bears bounced back the next day to beat host Spring Hill, 73–72, with Bowman playing a key role. Not only did he lead Baylor with twenty points, but Bowman also hit a baseline jumper with thirty seconds remaining to give Baylor a one-point lead. Then he went to the free-throw line and calmly made two shots with four seconds left to put the Bears in front, 73–70, and ice the win (there was no three-point line in college basketball until the 1986–87 season, so a three-point advantage with four seconds to go was a virtually insurmountable lead in 1967).

It had been an uneven beginning for Baylor, which went into 1968 with a 6–3 record. But Bowman, Gatewood, and Sibley had shown how much they could contribute to a Baylor team that included experienced upperclassmen in Thorpe, Kibbe, Eddie Frazier, and Randy Thompson.

"We were feeling good," Kibbe said. "I think we were picked last at the beginning of the year in the Southwest Conference. We weren't overconfident. But there was a good feeling in practice after we won a game. You could see through Coach Menefee that he was extremely happy that we had kind of melded together and done as well as we had."

Kibbe had been a standout basketball player at Dallas Hillcrest High School through his eleventh-grade year. But an injury during his senior year of high school kept him off the radar of college programs. He enrolled at Baylor and had assistant basketball coach Carroll Dawson for freshman physical education. Kibbe had already inquired about trying out for the Bears basketball program. A pick-up game in P.E. class, in which he and Dawson were on opposing teams and guarded each other, solidified his status. Dawson told him to come on out to practice on October 15.

Although the Cubs had seven freshmen on scholarship in Kibbe's freshman year, he worked his way into the starting lineup. In that way, the freshman squads of the day allowed for players to ascend within a program, as Sibley and Croucher found out a couple of years later.

By the time Bowman and Sibley were sophomores, they had become close friends, united in their dedication to their craft on the basketball court. Leading up to the start of practice, they would spend Friday nights in the weight room. Sibley had been given a partial scholarship at the beginning of the 1967–68 school year that covered his books and allowed him access to the athletic dining hall, right across from Martin Hall. But he wasn't content. He wore ankle weights around campus and would have Bowman climb on his back for a heavy jog up three flights of stairs at the dorm.

The work paid off. Sibley led Baylor in scoring at 16.6 points per game through nonconference play that fall. Gatewood had shown the ability to light up the scoreboard, but Sibley was more consistent.

"Sibley was a very intelligent basketball player," Bowman said. "He could know a guy's weakness and he would exploit it. Gatewood was a scorer, pure and simple. When we got to the point where we needed a basket, Coach Menefee would say, 'look, this is what we're going to do.' He was going to try to get Gatewood the ball in a position where Gatewood was comfortable. He never said, 'Tommy, I need you to do this,' because that was not my thing."

Menefee recognized how much Sibley brought to the table and put the sophomore from Houston on full scholarship going into the spring of 1968, giving him equal status with Bowman and Gatewood.

Meanwhile, Sibley was learning more and more about his friend and teammate from Athens. Living in a dorm full of young men who are granted more freedom than they've ever had before means seeing the entire spectrum of lifestyle choices. Sibley noticed the laziness of some guys who never bothered to keep up with the most basic housekeeping in their rooms. But every couple of days Bowman would have his bed made up with fresh linens, easily accessible from the dorm laundry service. Although Bowman admits he didn't quite live up to Madea's standards for church attendance, Sibley recalls rolling out of bed most Sundays just in time to get lunch at the dining hall and seeing Bowman, having returned from church, in his Sunday best and finishing up a meal.

"That's why I think Tommy was such a great thing for Baylor University," Sibley said. "He's religious and he's getting up and going to church. . . . He was that type of person. Much more fastidious than I was."

In less than a year and a half, Bowman had grown from a kid hiding out at his parents' house the week before he went to college to a man with a sense of the world. He was involved in Baylor campus life through his teammates and was also engaged with his fellow Black students as they made their way to church together on Sundays.

Bowman also made a point of reaching back out to James Cash at TCU. Cash played his first varsity season for the Horned Frogs in 1966–67, and soon he and Bowman would be competing against each other.

"I got an automobile my sophomore year. I would occasionally drive up to Fort Worth on Saturday and spend a little time with him, maybe even spend the night, and then come back to Waco on Sunday," Bowman said. "We developed a relationship. It was the fact that he was a Black basketball player in the Southwest Conference and so was I."

TCU unveiled a statue of James Cash, the first African American basketball player in the SWC, at the beginning of the 2022 23 basketball season.

Photo by Chad Conine

8
James Cash

Cash House at Harvard Business School sits just across Soldiers Field Road from a bend in the Charles River as it runs through the Harvard University campus in Cambridge, Massachusetts. The building, formerly known as Glass House and one of the original twelve buildings of Harvard Business School, was renamed in 2020 in honor of James Ireland Cash Jr., the James E. Robinson Professor of Business Administration, Emeritus.

James Cash's No. 54 has been retired by TCU basketball. He's a member of the Texas Sports Hall of Fame. He was the first Black basketball player in the Southwest Conference and Harvard Business School's first tenured African American professor. Those are the types of credentials that lead to a man having a building named for him on the Harvard campus.

It's about as prestigious as a person can get.

On the other hand, on a warm July morning in the summer of 2022, James Cash was just another friendly, jovial man in his mid-seventies fresh off the golf course at Farm Neck Golf Club on Martha's Vineyard. Cash has become an avid golfer and, as such, has made an impact on the golf world.

That's what he does.

Cash can't seem to help getting involved and effecting progress. Before talking about transforming SWC basketball in the 1960s, during lunch in the Farm Neck Golf Club he described the work it took to turn The Country Club in Brookline, Massachusetts back into a major golf venue. It had been just over a month since Matt Fitzpatrick won the US Open at The Country Club. Cash, a member of the Brookline club who served on its advance planning committee, watched the tournament with pride and delight.

During his round on the golf course that morning, Cash had to spend a few minutes waiting around for a former president of the United States to make his way around the course.

There aren't too many people who can slow down this Horned Frog, though.

After graduating from TCU in 1969, Cash earned a master's degree in computer science and Doctor of Philosophy in management information systems and accounting from Purdue. He soon joined the Harvard faculty in 1976. Throughout his career as a Harvard Business School professor, he also served on the boards of such companies as Walmart, General Electric, and Microsoft, and nonprofits like The Smithsonian National Museum of African American History and Culture and the National Association of Basketball Coaches Foundation. He's a part owner of the Boston Celtics.

Given his stature in American business and northeastern United States society, it's a little hard to believe that Cash, once upon a time, was an enforcer within the walls of South Side Rec Center in Fort Worth.

Cash, who grew up in Fort Worth, had risen to prominence as a high school hoops prospect going into his senior year at I. M. Terrell High School. As a six-foot-six center, he was regarded as the top player in Texas and received between 100 and 200 scholarship offers. But Cash can't let this point of fact pass without a joke at his own expense.

"Unfortunately, I was the same year as Lew Alcindor, or Kareem," Cash said. "What I learned on my [recruiting] trips was I should get to a school *before* he went there as opposed to after. Nobody was really interested in me after."

It was a big decision choosing where to play college basketball. At first, Cash was drawn to Wichita State, where a former mentor named John Gibbs was an assistant coach. Cash said another Wichita State scout had singled him out as the top player from the state of Texas in the class of 1965. The Fort Worth high schooler took recruiting visits to Michigan, Louisville, and Texas Western, among others. He could've been a freshman at Texas Western the year the Miners defeated Kentucky for the national championship.

Something happened, though, that caught Cash's attention. One day in the summer of 1964, he was playing basketball at the South Side gym, which was open to athletes of all races but not for integrated games. White players played at one end, and Black players at the other end.

In walked a TCU player named Garvin Isaacs. He looked around and decided the best basketball in the place was at the end of the gym where the Black players held the court. Somehow he got in the game, but he had to pay the price.

"I was the captain, the person responsible for implementing the code," Cash said. "So Garvin comes down and starts playing, and I knock him into a brick wall to send a message that he shouldn't be down there. It had happened a couple times before, and most people got the message. Garvin got up and kept playing. A few minutes later he paid me back. So, we squared off."

Luckily, Robert Hughes noticed the brawl in the offing.

In that subtle-but-profound way that separates the famous from the truly great, Robert Hughes is a giant of the Texas basketball landscape. Hughes coached high school basketball in Fort Worth from 1958 to 2005. He guided Terrell to three state championships in the Prairie View Interscholastic League—the division for Black schools prior to integration in Texas—and led Fort Worth Dunbar to two UIL state titles. Hughes retired as the United States' winningest high school coach with 1,333 victories and entered the Naismith Memorial Basketball Hall of Fame in 2017.

Much like Muhammad Ali, Abe Lemons, and Yogi Berra, Hughes was an intense competitor who also possessed a particular way with words. In the spring of 2003, when the Dunbar Flying Wildcats were on their way to the Class 4A state championship, Hughes set the national record with his 1,275th career coaching victory. Dunbar defeated Fort Worth Polytechnic for the historic win, and afterward a media throng gathered in an interview room at TCU's Daniel-Meyer Coliseum.

"Hot dog and hallelujah," Hughes told the assembled print and television reporters, including the *Fort Worth Star-Telegram*. "Our main focus was to win the district championship. That got inter-twined with this record. I tried to play it all season, like it wasn't there, but [the media] let them know everything about it, A to Z."

Hughes was relaxed and friendly with the media—an easy, juicy quote. That was a departure from his sideline demeanor. The tall and slender Hughes had a hawk-like stare and sporadically raised his voice to demand the utmost hustle from players and precise exe-cution of his team's game plan. He was very demanding, but Cash said if a player made it to his senior year, he had earned Hughes's respect and was treated like a lieutenant rather than a private.

When Cash and Isaacs faced off with each other, ready to raise their fists over the right to play in a summertime pick-up basketball game, Hughes was on top of it and quickly intervened. Looking back, Cash realized how a brawl in the gym could have had far-reaching consequences. Terrell ultimately won the PVIL state title in 1965, but the season could have gone down the drain with disciplinary actions if Cash had thrown a punch at the newcomer in the gym.

"So [Hughes] intervened quickly and talked to Garvin, realized that Garvin had grown up in an integrated environment and didn't understand," Cash said. "So [Hughes] turned to me and said, 'Let him play.'"

It's hard to unpack why near throw downs so often resulted in tight friendships in those days. It also happened with Tommy Bowman and David Sibley and Bowman and David Croucher. Whatever the explanation, Isaacs played basketball that day and befriended Cash.

When Terrell's season started later that year, Isaacs tracked the high school team and followed them to games all over the Dallas/Fort Worth metroplex. Cash said he knew some of the places his team played would be dangerous for outsiders coming into the gym. In such cases, he would warn his parents not to come. And then he would look up into the stands and see Isaacs sitting there, the only white person in the crowd.

Cash began to strongly consider TCU as his college destination, very much aware that it would mean becoming the first African American basketball player in the Southwest Conference. His friendship with Isaacs was a major bullet point in the pros column.

"As I thought about integrating the conference and what might happen and that type of stuff, I thought having a guy, first of all that was that crazy and courageous but has shown that level of interest in me as a person, would be a big factor in where I should go," Cash said. "I knew Garvin was going to be a teammate for at least one year. I knew that he would have my back on campus."

Since his college days, Cash has very much branched out from his Texas roots, but he chose to stay in his hometown for college because he knew what that decision would mean. Cash was a local high school hero in Fort Worth, but he was still a Black man crossing a well-established line.

A year before Bowman experienced racial hostility in road games as a freshman at Baylor, Cash met it head on in TCU's freshman games. He remembers some of the junior college road games being especially scary.

"There were places that had never had a Black athlete in the gym before," Cash said. "Just total lack of exposure, and what some people thought was fun was harassment."

Both Bowman and Cash played games in the Deep South when they reached the varsity level. In his book *Benching Jim Crow*, Charles H. Martin reported that Cash's nose was broken in an on-court altercation in Mobile, Alabama. Cash remembered the trip to the Alabama Classic for the way his teammates stood up for him.

"I don't know if this happened to Tommy, but my teammates refused to eat at a place because they were going to make me come through the back door," Cash said. "We ended up not staying at the place that had been booked because of the same thing."

Such cultural tug of wars took place all over the SWC and SEC states. One night in Fort Worth, the Baylor basketball team was headed into a nightclub called the Cellar Door when Bowman got a bad hit off the bouncer.

"We were like, 'Come on. This could be kind of exciting and fun,'" Sibley said. "About that time, the doorman said, 'We're full,' as people are coming from behind us and going in. I looked at Tommy and he kind of shook his head. So we went over to the TCU campus, he and I, and talked to Cash."

Bowman said he remembers Cash having a lot of friends and being kind of a big man on campus at TCU. That's one of the reasons he liked to drive up to Fort Worth and hang out on the weekend from time to time.

Having local ties helped Cash feel at ease in college. His acumen in the classroom, where he specialized in mathematics, played a key role as well. Throughout his career, Cash combined a sharp mind for numbers with pragmatism in business. He looks back on his specific abilities as important tools in fitting in.

"I didn't realize what a blessing it was that what I chose to major in was math," Cash said. "A lot of the folks, especially Black athletes, that had trouble in the classroom were in what I call qualitative courses as opposed to courses that were science based. The nice thing about the courses that I had was that it was like playing sports in the sense that there's a score and you could figure out who won. They can do a lot of other qualitative assessments but, at the end, it's either correct or not. For most of the classes that I was in, the fact that I could demonstrate that I knew what I was doing kind of took care of it."

There was some resistance to Buster Brannon recruiting the Terrell standout. *Benching Jim Crow* notes that one member of TCU's Board of Trustees resigned when the basketball program signed

Cash. But some members of the TCU faculty had shown a commitment to Cash's community before he enrolled there.

"A couple of professors at TCU, before Blacks were permitted to go to class on the TCU campus, came off of campus to run courses for Black teachers in the Fort Worth Independent School District," Cash said. "One of those teachers was my mother. I had this interesting impression of TCU as a result of those people deciding to go against the social norm, coming off and teaching these Black school teachers."

Ultimately, Cash's college decision didn't hinge on the potential for personal or team glory. He made a conscious decision to break the SWC color barrier at a place that could help him through it.

Even so, there was a bit of glory ahead.

Baylor varsity basketball coach Bill Menefee (center) talks with Tommy Bowman (right) and Steve Bartels (left).

Courtesy of Baylor Athletics via the Texas Collection

9
Sophomore Season
SWC Play, 1968

Whether college sports fans realize it or not, a big part of the attraction is the potential for breakout stars. That's why the recruiting of high school prospects is such a popular corner of the social media landscape in the mid-twenty-first century. We love to imagine how an up-and-coming player will fit into a squad and how he might shape the success of our team for years to come.

When a player not only lives up to those fantasies but shows himself or herself to be a frontline college athlete as soon as he or she steps onto the court or field, the excitement proliferates. He or she is contributing to winning, creating highlight plays, and giving fans a reason to buy tickets. But because the athlete is just bursting onto the scene, opponents might not have had time to uncover weaknesses, nor learn just how many ways the young player might be able to burn them.

As 1968 began, the Baylor player who logically fit the description of "breakout star" might have been Larry Gatewood. He was an All-American as a senior at Oklahoma City Northwest High School in 1966. Baylor landed him as a legacy recruit, and he proved himself by averaging twenty-six points for the Cubs freshman team in 1966–67. On the varsity, Baylor coach Bill Menefee deployed Gatewood as a sixth man during the 1967–68 season and he produced in the role. He came off the bench and scored twenty-four points in the Bears' Southwest Conference-opening victory over SMU on January 3, 1968 at Moody Coliseum in Dallas.

Baylor sent an early signal by beating the Mustangs on the road to begin its conference schedule. SMU had started very slowly, winning just once and losing eight games in nonconference play. But the Mustangs were the defending SWC champs.

"I still recall we were picked to finish last back before this season started, and SMU was picked on up the line a way," Menefee told *Tribune-Herald* sportswriter Jim Montgomery ahead of the first contest of 1968.

Gatewood made an immediate impact in his SWC debut. Menefee inserted him into the game with just five minutes gone off the clock. The Oklahoman responded with eight quick points and sparked Baylor to a 43–29 advantage at halftime.

"Larry Gatewood came in smoking hot, zip-zip-zip, points when we needed points," Menefee was quoted in a *Tribune-Herald* follow-up article.

Tommy Bowman scored twelve points in the second half to finish with fourteen versus SMU. Probably more importantly, he grabbed a team-high thirteen rebounds. Add in David Sibley's ten points, and the sophomore class was leading the charge.

Russell Kibbe, a senior, scored thirteen points to aid in Baylor's double-digit win over the Mustangs. He and classmate Ed Thorpe both fought through injuries, which created a peaks-and-valleys final year of college ball for each of them.

Kibbe said they could see that the sophomores were going to play a major part for Baylor. The roles were foreshadowed through offseason pick-up games and established in practice. If any upperclassmen were disappointed that their playing time was being usurped, Kibbe said they didn't have much defense. The sophomores were good, and Bowman in particular.

"The biggest impression on me was some sportswriter wrote after a game that Tommy played like he had jets in his heels," Kibbe said. "That stuck with me the rest of my life. Jets in his heels."

Gatewood could put the ball in the basket, no doubt. He was a top-notch shooter and one of those bygone legends who can only pine about having had the three-point line to boost his stats. He kept scoring for the Bears.

But Bowman was becoming Baylor's breakout star, and the Bears were attracting attention locally.

Baylor hosted Texas Tech on January 6. The *Tribune-Herald*'s game story began: "Before a large, chilled and delighted audience of 4,200 fans at Heart O' Texas Coliseum . . ." and went on with the details of the Bears' 64–50 victory. Kibbe and Randy Thompson were the leading scorers with seventeen and fifteen points. Bowman had nine points and a team-best ten rebounds.

The Bears stayed home for two more January games on either side of fall semester final exams. Baylor kept up its early SWC hot streak against Arkansas on January 9. Bowman scored eighteen points with nine rebounds, and the Bears beat the Razorbacks, 80–69. Thorpe was high-point man with twenty-one.

Baylor went into its exams on a four-game winning streak and tied with Texas for the SWC lead at 3–0. After a sixteen-day break, the Bears eased back into competition by crushing Tarleton State, 101–67, at Marrs McLean Gym in their final nonconference matchup of the season.

Menefee was hopeful that the lopsided win over Tarleton meant his team wasn't suffering from any post-exams rust. Whether it did or didn't, Baylor traveled to Fort Worth to play TCU two days later.

It was the first time two integrated SWC teams met in basketball, with Bowman going for Baylor and James Cash for TCU. However, not much was made of the milestone in newspaper reports either leading up to the game or in the game stories. The *Fort Worth Star-Telegram* did note that the game was televised throughout Texas.

The Horned Frogs, behind six-foot-five forward Mickey McCarty, halted the Bears' winning streak. The *Star-Telegram* featured a photo on its sports cover that showed McCarty going over Bowman for two of his thirty-six points.

Bowman said he developed a knack in college for positioning himself to rebound the basketball. By midway through his sophomore year, he knew he was either taller, quicker, or could jump higher—or a combination thereof—to beat just about anyone to the ball. That didn't apply to McCarty.

"I remember playing against Mickey McCarty up in Fort Worth," said the seventy-three-year-old Bowman, standing up and pantomiming boxing out an opponent in the lane. "It didn't matter about getting position on him. He was so big and strong. I can remember Mickey McCarty on my back. I'm blocking him out, and the goal is here. I'm down in a position where I can hold on, I think, and McCarty would just scoop me right out of the damn court. Mickey McCarty was like six foot five, and weighed 250 pounds, but it was just mass muscle."

Along with scoring thirty-six, McCarty pulled in a game-best sixteen rebounds. The Horned Frogs won the first of the season series against Baylor, 99–86. That put TCU in a three-way tie for first place in the SWC with Baylor and Rice, all of which had won three games and lost once.

But losing to the Horned Frogs seemed to serve as a spark for Baylor. The Bears followed up with three key victories over Rice, Texas A&M, and Texas, all by double digits.

Menefee astutely recognized Bowman's defensive ability and how it could be used for maximum impact in the Bears' game plan against Rice. The Owls came to Heart O'Texas Coliseum led by Larry Miller, a six-foot-three forward who was averaging twenty-one points. Bowman said Menefee did an excellent job of describing how an opponent would try to attack Baylor. The Bears coach outlined a plan for Bowman to be one step ahead of Miller all night, keeping the Rice star from even getting a shot to the basket most of the time.

Bowman was taller than Miller. Bowman was quicker than Miller. Bowman could jump higher than Miller. And as the game wore on, Bowman knew he was getting in his opponent's head. He sensed that the Owls' star was so frustrated that he wanted to hurl a racial slur but stopped short. "He was a nice guy," Bowman said. At the end of the night, Miller had gone one-for-six from the field, made his only free-throw attempt, and finished with three points.

"From that point, I decided if I could be the best defensive player on this team, I'm always going to have a spot in the starting five," Bowman said. "As it turned out, I did. In retrospect, I wish I had put a little more emphasis on scoring because I could've scored more points at Baylor. That was not that important to me."

Bowman contributed sixteen points as the Bears thumped Rice, 70–52. Kibbe led the way with twenty-two, and Thorpe also pitched in sixteen.

Soaring Baylor, once again alone at the top of the SWC standings, went to College Station next and claimed a 77–67 victory over Texas A&M. Kibbe scored twenty-two, and Bowman posted a double-double with seventeen points and eleven rebounds despite picking up his fourth foul early in the second half.

Baylor returned to Waco for a showdown with second-place Texas on February 6. The Bears' fan base was swelling as they sat atop the conference standings. A reported 5,000 came out for the Rice game the previous week, and, on a Tuesday night, 6,200 showed up for the Baylor-Texas clash.

Bowman, who finished with just four points, nailed a twenty-foot jump shot with just under sixteen minutes remaining. The basket put the Bears in front, 40–38, after they had trailed by three points at halftime. Baylor never fell behind in the contest after that Bowman basket and won, 74–58. Kibbe, becoming a points machine, had a game-high twenty-four. Sibley added seventeen, and Gatewood made his presence felt with fifteen.

After beating the Horns, Baylor had won eight of its last nine games. The Bears then headed for Houston and one of Bowman's shining moments.

Not the least of its accomplishments, Baylor's basketball team had captured the attention of legendary *Tribune-Herald* sports editor Dave Campbell.

In his later years, Campbell actively followed basketball, especially Baylor's juggernaut Lady Bears. But scrolling through the sports pages of the 1960s, Campbell was most likely writing about SWC football, whatever the calendar said. Nonetheless, he made the trip to Houston to report on the Baylor-Rice game.

"In the game's last decisive seconds, the coolest of the cool was acrobatic Tommy Bowman," Campbell wrote.

With Baylor leading by a single point, Bowman fought to gather in a loose ball under the Owls' basket and was fouled in the process with eleven seconds on the clock. Campbell noted that Bowman masked any nerves he might have been feeling as he "swished through" a pair of free throws. Rice countered with a last second bucket, but it merely made the final score razor thin as Baylor won, 59–58. Campbell penned: "At the final buzzer, Bowman had the ball securely in his mitts, which was appropriate."

Even more than fifty years removed from the game, Kibbe corroborated Campbell's analysis.

"Those two pressure free throws really won the game for us," Kibbe said. "[Bowman has] probably dealt with pressure all his life. Not many people go through it where if you make these shots you win or lose. That impressed me greatly."

Campbell recognized Bowman's effort in several ways, including interviewing the sophomore forward. Bowman might've appeared calm and collected, but he was actually very aware of the potential consequences of a missed free throw. "I was thinking if I missed those shots I was going to be the goat of the game," Bowman told Campbell. "I couldn't have gone back to Waco. No way."

The Bears' win at Rice extended their lead to two games in the SWC table as then-second-place Arkansas lost on the same day against TCU.

It's too obscure to go down as the jinx of all jinxes, but Associated Press sportswriter Harold V. Ratliff put a doozy on Baylor as it entered the week of Valentine's Day, 1968: "Baylor's Bears . . . could virtually sew up the Southwest Conference basketball championship this week."

Baylor took a 14–4 overall record and 7–1 conference mark into a matchup with Texas in Austin. Injuries started to nag the Bears, and they lost that edge of momentum that is so crucial in the slog of conference play where everyone knows you as well as you know them.

Bowman had a stellar game individually at Texas's Gregory Gym. He scored nineteen points and grabbed thirteen rebounds, leading Baylor in both categories. But the Longhorns had an excellent shooting night and avenged their sixteen-point loss a week earlier in Waco with a 79–65 victory on their home court. Thorpe and Kibbe combined for just nine points, perhaps feeling the pains that would knock each of them out of the lineup in key moments the rest of the way.

Thorpe missed the next two games as Texas A&M came to Waco and claimed a four-point win and SMU followed by beating Baylor by seven. Bowman scored twenty-five points in the loss to the Mustangs. But his good night on the offensive end was actually a bad sign. The Bears were best when Kibbe led them in scoring and Bowman, Sibley, or Gatewood—or, even better, a combination—filled in behind.

Kibbe came out of the SMU game with a knee injury and missed the next one as Baylor traveled to Lubbock to play Texas Tech. The trip out west presented another challenge for Bowman, who hadn't been there yet. The Red Raiders were not on the freshman schedule. Menefee warned Bowman that the Texas Tech home crowd usually applauded the visiting players during introductions but picked one player to snub in an attempt at psychological warfare.

"I figured I'd be that one player and sure enough I was," Bowman said. "When they introduced me that night, you could hear a pin drop. But I was kind of prepared for that. I don't think that had anything to do with me being Black, red, green, or gold."

Bowman tipped in a shot with eleven seconds remaining in the second half as Baylor tried to rally from a late eight-point deficit. But the Red Raiders held on to a 65–63 win, handing the Bears their fourth consecutive defeat.

However, Baylor had fallen just one spot in the standings. Texas moved up to first place with an 8–4 record, and the Bears, Aggies, and Horned Frogs were knotted up in second, a game back.

On February 27, Baylor went to Arkansas and claimed a 71–64 victory, using a stalling tactic at the end of the second half to preserve the win. That same Tuesday night, TCU defeated front-running Texas, 71–65, and Texas Tech beat Texas A&M, 83–81. That set the stage for Baylor and TCU—Bowman and Cash—to play for at least a share of the SWC championship the following Saturday.

✦ ✦ ✦

The Heart O' Texas Coliseum stands as one of the most mocked basketball arenas in the history of big-time college basketball. It looks like a gigantic barn and in many ways functioned better in that capacity. The arena, renamed the Extraco Events Center, still hosts multiple rodeo events each year at the time of this writing. In its days as a basketball facility, the HOT Coliseum was poorly lit and lacked some basic athletics amenities. The teams used portable buildings situated behind the grandstands as makeshift locker rooms. Eventually, Carroll Dawson left Baylor because he grew tired of trying to recruit to the out-of-place arena. Baylor opened the Ferrell Center in the fall of 1988, and it eventually housed the rise of both the Bears and Lady Bears basketball teams.

Even so, the HOT Coliseum, more than fifteen years old in the spring of 1968, played host to the de facto SWC men's basketball championship game. Arkansas defeated Texas on the same day, knocking the Longhorns out of the running for the title and leaving the Bears and Horned Frogs to battle it out. The *Tribune-Herald* reported a crowd of over-capacity 8,100 in attendance for the Baylor-TCU matchup.

A couple of days after the game, *Star-Telegram* columnist Galyn Wilkins told an old tale about how SMU had once prepared to play at the dark and dingy HOT Coliseum by dimming the lights in its own gym. Wilkins gave an unflattering description of Baylor basketball's home arena: "Unquestionably, it's a functional, even luxurious home for prize cattle during the county fair but Baylor's basketball coliseum is a forbidding arena in which to fight for a conference championship."

Despite the Coliseum's shortcomings, Baylor and TCU engaged in a thriller. The two teams traded the lead thirteen times during the contest's first thirty minutes. Bowman finished with sixteen points to lead Baylor.

But injuries flared up again for the Bears. Kibbe said he tried to make a go of it, but Menefee could tell the senior guard wasn't right. Kibbe spent most of the night watching from the bench. Thorpe played well, and well into the second half. But a leg injury caused him to come out of the game with 13:36 remaining and the score tied at forty-two. Thorpe briefly tried to get back in but didn't last long.

TCU made its move in the final ten minutes behind Cash, who might never have been better. He hit a crucial hook shot in the lane and was fouled by Bowman with about five minutes left. By completing a three-point play, Cash thwarted a Baylor rally and pushed the Horned Frogs' advantage to six points.

It was the free-throw shooting that everyone remembers.

"James Cash was one of the worst free-throw shooters in the whole wide world," Bowman said. "At the end of the game we were trying to catch up, and Cash would step up to the free-throw line like it was just routine for him. When he needed to make them, he made them. I'll give him credit for that."

The *Star-Telegram* noted that Cash was the team's worst free-throw shooter, and yet the game story also described how the TCU junior felt confident from the stripe on that day. Cash went seven-for-seven on free throws as he scored a game-high twenty-five points. Both of the newspaper beat writers described Cash as the difference in the game as the Horned Frogs won, 72–65, to claim the SWC title.

"I can't believe it . . . can't believe we're the conference champions," Cash told *Star-Telegram* reporter Dick Moore.

In years to come, such a showdown as the one in which Baylor and TCU engaged for the SWC title on the Bears' home floor would merely be a prelude to the postseason. Starting in 1976, both teams traveled to the conference tournament and, given their respective records, could have hoped for an NCAA Tournament automatic berth or an at-large invitation to the Big Dance. However, in 1968 there was no conference tourney. TCU earned the SWC's spot in the 1968 NCAA Tournament as the conference champion. Baylor's season ended with the loss on its home court.

The Horned Frogs defeated Kansas State, 77–72, in the Midwest Region semifinal. Houston, as was the Cougars' habit in those days, eliminated the SWC champs, 103–68, to get to the Final Four.

Cash's Horned Frogs and Bowman's Bears would play two more times the next season when Cash was a senior. Both men went on to successful careers, as did many of the players and coaches involved on that most glorious of hoops nights at the HOT Coliseum.

Then one day in the early 2000s, Cash traveled to Houston on Boston Celtics business. He stuck his head in Carroll Dawson's Houston Rockets office to say hello. Dawson, ever the competitor, immediately expressed his disbelief that Cash had gone seven-for-seven from the free-throw line on March 2, 1968.

"I hadn't seen Carroll Dawson for decades," Cash said. "I walked in his office, that was the first thing out of his mouth. That was literally the funniest thing that has happened to me in my life."

Tommy Bowman signs an autograph for young fan Brent Rasner outside
of the locker room at the Heart O' Texas Coliseum.

Courtesy of Baylor Athletics via the Texas Collection

Tommy Bowman and his wife Jackie, pictured with their children Tommy II and Krystal, have been married for more than fifty years.

Courtesy of the Bowman Family

10
Meeting Jackie

All of our lives float on the current of time, either along with or through the milestone events that define the years in which we live. There are elections and Super Bowls and March Madnesses that transcend others of their kind. But those are scheduled events that can be anticipated and expected to be larger than life even if they eventually turn out to be ordinary.

It's the unplanned that really shakes us. COVID-19 lasted a long time, prompting conversations and even shaping ideologies. September 11, 2001 was sudden and earthshaking.

David Koresh's Branch Davidians drew the nation's attention to Waco with their shootout with the ATF on February 28, 1993, and then again when their compound was set ablaze and burned fifty days later. That event defined Waco for a generation, but a person could live in the town and feel no more connection to that odd and tragic story than any other item in the twenty-four-hour news cycle.

The pulse of the 1960s was raging in 1968 as so many of the events that we talk about when we talk about the 1960s took place. In college basketball, Houston and UCLA played the Game of the Century in the Astrodome on January 20. Elvin Hayes and Houston defeated Lew Alcindor and UCLA, 71–69, in the first college basketball game to be broadcast nationally in primetime. They met again at the end of March in the national semifinals when UCLA took decisive revenge, 101–69. Then the Bruins dispensed with North Carolina in the final, 78–55, for their second consecutive national championship. In this case, at least, sports reflected the back-and-forth of the era—wonders and tragedies and controversies battling for headlines.

Martin Luther King Jr. was assassinated in Memphis on April 4. The nation mourned but also rioted. Two months later, Robert Kennedy also died by an assassin's bullet, cutting short his bid for the Democratic nomination for president.

On May 2, Bill Russell served as player-coach and led the Boston Celtics to a clinching win over the Los Angeles Lakers in the NBA Finals. Russell scored twelve points and grabbed nineteen rebounds while Celtics guard John Havlicek poured in forty points with seven assists. Lakers Elgin Baylor and Jerry West combined for fifty points in a losing effort. It was the sixth time that Russell's Celtics had beaten the Lakers in the Finals since 1959.

The Beatles released "Hey Jude" on August 26. Two days later, violence erupted at the Democratic National Convention in Chicago.

Arthur Ashe claimed the US Open tennis title on September 9 and became the first Black man to lift a Grand Slam individual championship trophy.

All the while, the war in Vietnam slogged on, featuring in television news broadcasts and weighing on the minds of potential draftees.

+ + +

Tommy Bowman concedes he felt pretty good about himself following his first varsity season of college basketball in the spring of 1968, with good reason. Bowman earned first-team All-Southwest Conference recognition from the Associated Press, joining Mickey McCarty from TCU, Billy Arnold and Gary Overbeck from Texas, Ronnie Peret from Texas A&M, and Lynn Phillips from SMU. The *Waco Tribune-Herald* went a step further and declared Bowman as the SWC Sophomore of the Year (the AP team didn't name individual honors).

Bowman averaged fifteen points according to the chart that ran along with the *Tribune-Herald*'s all-conference article. He was the second lowest scorer on the first team, but he wasn't counted on to be the Bears' leader in that category. He also came in near double digits in rebounding and was Baylor's best defender.

Bowman had proven himself and gained confidence. But it wasn't something he necessarily took in stride.

"I can't believe the honors I received," Bowman said. "I couldn't believe I was at Baylor, first of all. I couldn't believe that I was competing with these guys from Dallas and Houston and these big schools. It took me awhile to get acclimated to that was who I was and what I was doing."

While he grappled with it, Bowman had caught the eye of a few people around Waco, including a young lady at the First Baptist Church. Tommy Bowman first met Jackie Sallard in Sunday School, and their courtship unfolded from there.

One Sunday after Bowman had gone to Sunday School at New Hope Baptist Church with his friends Choice Richardson and Charles Houston, they talked him into going to services at First Baptist. Then they told Tommy they had been invited to lunch at Jackie Sallard's house.

Bowman started to decline. After all, he had a free lunch and a good one waiting for him at Martin Hall. He remembered it this way: "Choice said, 'Come on, Tommy, the only reason she invited us is because she wanted you over there.' So I went, and the next thing I know I had a date with Jackie and then we kind of got close."

Whether Bowman knew it or not, everything had been mapped out by Jackie's mother, Nell Sallard, whom the extended family called "Sister." Jackie's younger cousin Nell Murphy Wilson watched it happen and remembers how her aunt and namesake influenced the situation. On the day that Tommy was invited to lunch, Sister told the younger kids to be on their best behavior. Nell Murphy Wilson said her cousin Jackie focused almost all of her attention on school and church. Jackie said she remembers meeting Tommy and thinking he was "a nice guy and cool guy." But Sister wasn't going to let Tommy get away.

"When Jackie's mother laid eyes on Tommy, she knew," Nell Murphy Wilson said. "She even told Jackie, 'That's going to be your husband one day.' Sister was determined. . . . But I think their relationship and meeting was ordained by God. I truly do because he fit into our family very well."

1968 EAST
Kneeling (l.-r.): Bob Dillow, Joe Lanning, Tom Bowman, Randy Thompson, Ri...
Standing: S.I.D. David Cawood, Asst. Coach Carroll Dawson, Larry Gatewood,
Bartels and trainer David Huffstetler

...INA CHAMPIONS
...Scallorn, Eddie Frazier and David Sibley
...Schlueter, Tom Freidman, David Nelson, Dr. Leo Jenkins, Coach Bill Menefee, Steve

11
Junior Season
Fall of 1968

If basketball season wanted to quietly sneak in the back door, December of 1968 was a good time to do it. Baylor had just fired football coach/athletic director John Bridgers and began a coaching search that would put Bill Beall in that office. The Texas Longhorns had just beaten Texas A&M for the Southwest Conference football title and would face Tennessee in the Cotton Bowl. Texas was ascending to a three-year stretch of sharing a piece of the national championship vote. Richard Nixon was elected president a month earlier. USC's O. J. Simpson had just won the Heisman, and Elvis launched a comeback with a one-hour NBC special on the same night that the Bears basketball team tipped off their season.

Jim Montgomery once again manned the Baylor hoops beat for the *Waco Tribune-Herald*. His season preview included a headshot of Tommy Bowman and touted Bowman's status as returning SWC sophomore of the year. However, the expectations for the Bears' season got buried by everything else going on in sports or otherwise. If followers were hopeful or if experts were predicting that Baylor would build on its second-place finish in the conference race during the previous spring, it didn't show up in newspaper copy.

The Bears' preseason practice had been interrupted by injuries and illness. David Sibley had an abdominal strain. Bowman caught the flu the week before the season-opener against Texas Lutheran.

Even so, Baylor launched without much problem, rolling over the Lutherans, 73–52. Bowman scored eleven despite foul trouble. Senior guard Eddie Frazier, a bit player the previous two seasons on the Baylor varsity, scored the first basket of the campaign and ended the opening game with twelve. Texas Lutheran had played six games before arriving at the Heart O' Texas Coliseum, while Baylor was trying to find its identity after Russell Kibbe and Ed Thorpe graduated. Yet the Bears didn't have too much trouble with the Bulldogs.

Menefee knew his team was still a work in progress. "I'm not bitterly unhappy with this game. I've had teams play well and lose," he told Montgomery.

Two days later, the Bears traveled to New Orleans for games on back-to-back nights against Loyola and Tulane.

In the record book, it appears that everything was going smoothly. After winning their season opener, the Bears added victories against the Wolf Pack and the Green Wave in the Big Easy that weekend. Against Loyola, Gatewood scored nineteen, Frazier added eighteen, and Bowman had ten points and ten rebounds in a 99–88 win.

Looking a little closer, the New Orleans trip had a shakier start. The game story from the win over Loyola, provided to the *Tribune-Herald* by an unnamed freelance sportswriter, mentioned that Baylor had been delayed four hours in Dallas because the players' bags didn't make it onto their airplane. Then, when the Bears arrived in New Orleans, the team had to change hotels. None of the Baylor players interviewed for this book remember the travel problems during the early-season nonconference road trip, and yet they were significant enough at the time to make the newspaper account. Lost bags can happen for a lot of reasons. But the need to change hotels? It's worth noting that less than three years earlier the American Football League All-Star Game relocated from New Orleans to Houston at the last minute because of racism that Black players encountered upon arriving in New Orleans. James Cash, who himself experienced racial discrimination in the Deep South around the same time, said he thinks it's likely that a hotel might have sent Baylor away because the Bears had a Black player.

One of the personality traits that helped Tommy Bowman persevere in his time at Baylor was that he didn't let things stick to him. He and Sibley laughed it off when a little girl morphed into a racial-slur-screaming demon at Texas A&M. Bowman didn't regard the deafening silence when his name was announced at Texas Tech as an act of passive aggression because he was African American.

Once when Bowman and some of his white friends, including Woody Rogers, drove out to Bellmead to a tavern called Lone Star Steakhouse, the restaurant refused to seat them. The group left. Rogers and Sibley, both of whom have remained in Waco throughout their lives, never ate there again despite the fact that Lone Star has persevered as a Bellmead establishment until the time of this writing.

Bowman thinks maybe some of the white Baylor football players avoided him in the dining hall, but he doesn't keep a mental list of names or any kind of specifics. And if a certain New Orleans hotel refused to accommodate Bowman and Baylor in December of 1968, he hasn't cataloged that in his memory either.

One thing is clear in the record, Bowman had a great game against Tulane. He scored twenty-four points to lead Baylor past the Green Wave, 82–80. Often when Bowman scored in the twenties, it was because the rest of Baylor's best offensive players faltered, and it resulted in a Bears loss. Not in this game. Gatewood added nineteen, including a basket with seven seconds remaining that proved to be the difference on the scoreboard.

Baylor returned home from New Orleans with a 3–0 record. Although it was a modest winning streak, it still signaled the program's best beginning in four years. New Mexico State halted that run, however, by winning 69–58 in Waco on December 14. Lou Henson's Aggies ended up ranked No. 12 in the nation at the end of the season after they lost to UCLA in the West regional semifinals in the NCAA Tournament. Guard Jimmy Collins scored twenty-six points to lead New Mexico State as Baylor searched for cohesion on the defensive end. Bowman had a double-double with fifteen points and twelve rebounds. Frazier once again led Baylor in scoring with eighteen.

The 2010s and 2020s version of the Baylor basketball team, having achieved prominence under head coach Scott Drew, plays in some of the nation's top showcase nonconference basketball tournaments—the Battle 4 Atlantis in the Bahamas, the Jimmy V Classic at Madison Square Garden, the Maui Invitational, etc. But early-season tournaments in college basketball have been the norm for a long time. According to Baylor basketball's media almanac, the Bears first played in such an event when they traveled to Oklahoma City for the All-College Tournament at New Year's in the 1936–37 season. That became an annual tradition for Baylor for the next fifteen years.

Menefee took his Baylor teams to back-to-back tournaments to finish 1968, traveling to the Bayou Holiday Classic in Lafayette, Louisiana and then the East Carolina Classic in Greenville, North Carolina. The trajectory of the team, and the momentum that would carry the Bears deep into SWC play, can be easily traced through their performance along the way.

Baylor opened the Bayou Holiday Classic by defeating Hawaii, 78–69. The Rainbows led late in the first half before Gatewood found his shooting touch from the field. He scored twenty-one to lead the Bears. Bowman didn't make a field goal until midway through the second half, but he heated up and finished with fifteen points to help Baylor pull away.

By holding off Hawaii, the Bears earned the chance to face host Southwestern Louisiana in the final of the four-team scrum. Alas, as often happens in basketball, once one team starts going to the free-throw line it's hard to keep it from becoming a parade. The home-standing Cajuns didn't have a great night percentage-wise from the foul stripe—they made a pedestrian seventy-one percent—but they got forty-five chances compared to seventeen shots for Baylor.

David Cawood, who went on to prominence as an NCAA administrator and helped to popularize the Final Four throughout the 1970s, 1980s, and 1990s, served as the Bears' sports information director during much of Bowman's career. He was quoted in the *Tribune-Herald*'s game story: "It was four, five, or six points most of the way, but whenever we got too close it was time to shoot free throws again. Three different times they shot five free throws in a row."

Gatewood scored thirty to lead Baylor, and Bowman added fifteen. But Eddie Frazier and fellow guard Randy Thompson fouled out midway through the second half, and Bowman and Sibley were hamstrung with four fouls each. Southwestern Louisiana claimed an 86–78 victory and its own tournament title.

The Bayou Holiday Classic finished on December 21, then the Bears had just five days to get home, celebrate Christmas and get to Greenville, North Carolina for the East Carolina Classic tournament beginning on December 26.

Baylor opened with William & Mary, which had a much shorter trip to Greenville, less than 200 miles from Williamsburg, Virginia. The Indians, as they were known before switching to the Tribe in the late 1970s, started faster than Baylor and led the Bears for much of the first half. But Baylor's defense played a leading role starting about eighteen minutes into the contest. The Bears held William & Mary scoreless for the final 2:21 of the half, allowing Baylor to surge to a 47–39 advantage at the break, and they would not relinquish the lead. Baylor's outstanding junior class led the way to an 81–68 win. Gatewood scored nineteen points, Bowman had eighteen, and Sibley added thirteen.

Of course, not all the teams in the East Carolina Classic were from Virginia, just the three that Baylor played in the event. Virginia Tech beat Delaware to reach the tournament semifinals against the Bears.

Gatewood scored twenty-four points as Baylor edged Virginia Tech. Yet it was Bowman whose headshot appeared alongside the *Tribune-Herald* game report with the caption, "Anchors BU Effort." The Bears had a less-than-blazing shooting night against the Gobblers, meaning their defense had to do the hard work. Bowman posted a double-double with twelve points and ten rebounds. More importantly, the game story noted he "anchored a stout defense by blocking several shots and intercepting two passes." Baylor led by nine at halftime, then persevered through a slow second half on the offensive end. Sibley, who finished with fourteen points, made a crucial free throw in the final minute, and Gatewood made two more as the Bears notched a 66–63 victory.

Baylor's second win in the tournament put the Bears in a late-night championship game versus Virginia. Although both programs have played major conference basketball for a long time and achieved a high level of success in the 2010s, their contest for the Eastern Carolina Classic title remained their only meeting going into the 2022–23 basketball season. Baylor fans have bragging rights over the Cavaliers in that sense as the championship game wasn't close for long. The Bears took an eleven-point lead to halftime and ultimately stomped on Virginia, 79–61.

Gatewood, settling into the leading role at least on offense for Baylor, claimed tournament MVP honors. He scored twenty-six in the final to average twenty-three in the event. Bowman had just eight points and eight rebounds in the championship game, but he made his impression felt and earned All-Tournament along with Gatewood.

Baylor's "Virginia State Championship" finished up on December 28, giving the Bears ten days to prepare to open SWC play at home against SMU. They had created momentum that would carry them through the next several weeks.

Tommy Bowman attempts a jump shot in a game versus SMU at the
Heart O' Texas Coliseum.

Courtesy of Baylor Athletics via the Texas Collection

12
Junior Season
SWC Play, 1969

Tommy Bowman was headed into a landmark year of his life on New Year's Day, 1969. He married Jackie, with David Sibley standing by his side as best man, on May 31. He and Jackie moved into an apartment near campus in the summer, and Tommy started his senior year of college in the fall. Like every other American man between nineteen and twenty-five years old, Bowman held his breath during the draft lottery that took place on December 1, 1969. He drew a high number as his birthday, May 9, was assigned 197. He wouldn't be called into service.

But when the year began, Bowman and his Baylor teammates focused on preparing for Southwest Conference play. A year after losing to TCU in the final game of the season and finishing second in the SWC, the Bears could no longer sneak up on their conference foes. And yet, they didn't take a step back.

Baylor hosted SMU on January 6 to start the league. The game drew a crowd of 5,500 to the Heart O' Texas Coliseum, according to Jim Montgomery's game story in the *Tribune-Herald*. Bears fans saw their team wander into foul trouble, which had been one of their few weak points so far in the season. Bowman, who had earned the reputation as Baylor's "defensive kingpin and chief rebounder," was whistled for his fourth foul early in the second half. Sibley, too, went to the bench with four fouls just a little bit after his buddy.

Bowman and Sibley came back in time to pull in vital rebounds in the final two minutes. Baylor couldn't convert those gained possessions into points, though. Sibley, Randy Thompson, and Eddie Frazier combined to miss five consecutive free throws, any one of which could have put a five-point game out of reach for the Mustangs.

Instead, the result came down to a simple misstep. SMU star guard Gene Phillips, who earned the *Tribune-Herald*'s Sophomore of the Year designation at season's end, attempted to drive the baseline with Baylor's Richard Scallorn guarding him. Phillips stepped out of bounds with two seconds left. He scored twenty-eight points in the contest but never got off his game-tying attempt. The Bears prevailed, 69–67.

Larry Gatewood once again led Baylor with twenty-five points. Bowman scored ten of Baylor's twelve points in the game's final eight minutes. He finished with thirteen points and eighteen rebounds, but his most valuable contribution might not have shown up in the game story or box score. Thompson said Bowman excelled at shutting down SMU's Bill Voight whenever the Bears played the Ponies. Voight averaged twenty points that season but managed just thirteen that night at the HOT Coliseum.

After beating SMU, Baylor had achieved its longest winning streak of the campaign and kept adding to it. The Bears traveled to Fort Worth three days later for a Friday game against TCU. James Cash, the hero of the Horned Frogs' conference-clinching win in Waco the previous March, made a crucial mistake this time around. With Baylor leading by one point and with nineteen seconds left in the second half, Cash reached and slapped the ball out of Bowman's hands as he was about to throw an in-bounds pass. By rule, that's a technical foul. Gatewood took the free throws and made them both to extend the Bears' lead to 67–64. Sibley added one more free throw with six seconds remaining to make the final margin 68–64 in Baylor's favor.

Gatewood finished with twenty points, Bowman added fifteen, and Sibley came in strong with eleven rebounds. The junior class led the way as the Bears floated into a thirteen-day break for fall semester exams riding a five-game winning streak.

Baylor kept the laughs going out of the break as they cruised past Tarleton State, 103–57, on January 23. Bowman had a double-double with fifteen points and sixteen rebounds. Pretty much all of the Bears players got in the scoring act. Baylor coach Bill Menefee commented that he believed the students in attendance wanted to see Baylor score 150, but the coach had been on the wrong end of that type of game too many times to take advantage of the visiting Texans.

Either way, Baylor's frolicking was short-lived.

Among the many amazing coincidences in sports history, it's hard to overlook the fact that Texas Tech and Baylor played in men's basketball national championship games in back-to-back NCAA Tournaments. The Red Raiders made the Final Four and ultimately fell to Virginia in overtime in the title game in 2019. After the 2020 tourney was canceled because of the national reaction to the oncoming COVID-19 pandemic, Baylor won the "Bubble" NCAA Tournament in 2021. What makes it so unbelievable is that Baylor and Texas Tech basketball have trudged along in the shadows in a football state for a century and, even beyond that, have been treated as second-class citizens in athletics by the likes of Texas and Texas A&M for most of their existence.

But the Bears vs. the Red Raiders has been a good rivalry in basketball, especially in the early twenty-first century. Entering the 2023–24 season, Baylor has won seven of the last ten meetings and both teams have been ranked much of the time.

And yet, Texas Tech has a significant upper hand in the all-time series. The Red Raiders established a twenty-game lead on the strength of long winning streaks against Baylor. Texas Tech went on runs of at least six consecutive wins over the Bears in the 1960s, 1970s, 1980s, 1990s, and 2000s. It's a testament to how much the Bowman-Gatewood-Sibley era accomplished in that Baylor went 4–2 versus the Red Raiders from 1968 to 1970.

On January 25, 1969, though, Texas Tech came to Waco and stopped Baylor's budding winning streak. The Bears had strung together six straight victories going back to the East Carolina Classic. However, they couldn't find the range from the free-throw line in their first SWC game back from final exams. *Tribune-Herald* sports editor Dave Campbell noted that Baylor players missed the front end of a one-and-one trip to the foul line on four different occasions. While Baylor was starving for a made free throw, Texas Tech feasted on sixteen consecutive good free shots.

"Against TCU we lined up and made them till the cows came home," Menefee bemoaned. "It's something you can't explain."

Bowman had a double-double against the Red Raiders, with fourteen points and twelve rebounds. He also made all four of his free-throw attempts. But Baylor, which was among the nation's top ten in free-throw percentage going in, connected on just twenty-two of thirty-two.

Baylor bounced back at the free-throw line and on the scoreboard in its next outing. The Bears' last eleven points came at the stripe as they defeated Arkansas, 74–72, on January 28 in Fayetteville.

The Bears stayed on the road four days later, playing Rice in Houston to start February. Baylor claimed a tense 71–68 victory that got under the skin of some Rice fans. Montgomery reported that a parliament of Owls supporters rushed the court after the final buzzer and charged at the officials. Referee Bob Smith "hurled one youth to the floor," and the striped shirts escaped with no further incident.

At that time, the possession arrow hadn't come along to decide tie balls (when two players from opposing teams take simultaneous possession of the ball). That's one hidden area where Bowman proved a key asset. He won a crucial jump ball against Rice with about half a minute remaining. Baylor made the most of the gained possession as Gatewood nailed a fourteen-foot jump shot that put the Bears in front, 69–68. The Owls couldn't get a good look in the final thirty seconds to retake the lead and Baylor, like the referees, got away unscathed.

The win in Houston put Baylor back on a winning streak and just a game behind Texas A&M in the SWC standings, in time for a Bears-Aggies showdown in Waco on February 4. According to Montgomery's gamer, the Baylor vs. Texas A&M basketball game drew 8,500 spectators to the HOT Coliseum on a Tuesday night, setting an arena attendance record. The crowd didn't go away disappointed.

The Aggies surged ahead by thirteen points early in the second half, but Baylor roared back behind guard Tom Friedman's hot shooting. Friedman scored fifteen points in the second half and played a leading role as the Bears rallied to tie the score at fifty-seven with seven minutes left. Texas A&M led by three with eighty seconds remaining, then Friedman connected on a running jump shot just outside the lane that made it a one-point game going into the final minute.

Baylor caught a break when the Aggies' Sonny Benefield broke from his team's stall tactic and launched a fifteen-footer. It missed, and Gatewood grabbed the rebound. Ultimately, Gatewood made two free throws with nineteen seconds on the clock to put the Bears in front. He also snatched the rebound when Benefield missed a last-second attempt.

The history books, including this one, will usher Bowman forward as Baylor's reluctant star in the late 1960s. However, Gatewood consistently lived up to the hype that surrounded him when he came to Baylor as a high school All-American. In this game against the SWC-leading Aggies, he was the man. He finished with twenty-four points and eleven rebounds, making many of the crucial plays for the Bears at the end in front of a huge crowd. Bowman did his thing, to be sure, notching fifteen points and eleven boards. But his efforts were definitely in a supporting role. Baylor also benefited from Texas A&M star forward Billy Bob Barnett fouling out of the game with 5:31 left in the second half.

Baylor took the momentum with them to Austin the following Saturday and used it to trample Texas by fourteen points. Bowman made a pair of free throws that put the Bears in front, 50–49, with 12:27 remaining, and Baylor never trailed after that. The Bears won, 71–57, which must have been a satisfying result for Bowman in particular. He scored nineteen points, but more importantly Baylor had overcome a Longhorn team with a tendency to annoy.

"When I played against the guys at Texas, they would try to play with your mind," said Bowman, who had just six rebounds in the win over Texas. "I even had them come up from behind me and grab my pants and actually put their hands there and hold me. That kind of threw me way off. Nobody had ever done anything like that before. I don't know if that was something they planned to do, but it was a couple of them. I thought, 'What the heck is going on here?' All my high school days and when I played at the Black high school, Fisher High School, when I played at Athens High School and then all the time I played at Baylor, nobody had ever done anything like that. I swatted their hands away because, can you imagine, you're in a position to get a rebound and all of a sudden somebody has got their hands on your shorts, pulling you down."

Shady tactics averted, Baylor reached the second week of February on a four-game winning streak that put the Bears at 14–3 on the season. That was enough for Baylor to achieve a program first. According to Baylor's media almanac, the Bears were ranked No. 19 in the nation after defeating Texas A&M and Texas during the first eight days of February, marking the first time they had entered the national poll.

Alas, the ranking proved to be short-lived. Rice came to Waco on February 11 and handed Baylor a two-point loss. The Bears apparently fell out of favor with the poll voters after that. Even another win over Texas on February 15 couldn't balance the scales.

Baylor's triumph versus the Horns at HOT Coliseum put Bowman in the center of the spotlight. Montgomery's report began, "Tommy Bowman was a master archer, targeting twenty-six points Saturday night and leading Baylor to a vital 63–58 victory over the Texas Longhorns." In defeating Texas in Waco, Baylor had earned a season sweep of a decent Horns team. The game story also noted that the win kept the Bears just a game behind SWC leader Texas A&M. As fate would have it, Baylor was scheduled to travel to College Station the following Tuesday.

Everyone associated with Baylor basketball in the 1960s who has lived to tell about it remembers the second Bears-Aggies game of

1969, even if some of the details have been blurred by time. It didn't turn out well for Baylor on the scoreboard. Although Texas A&M went on to win the SWC title, the Aggies didn't walk away from their home game against the Bears feeling too good about it either.

Texas A&M learned something from its loss in Waco two weeks earlier, and Shelby Metcalf made the lesson count. The Aggies built up a 37–25 lead late in the first half. They stiff-armed a Baylor run early in the second half and were easily protecting a double-digit margin when tensions overflowed and things got ugly.

Bears guard David Croucher made a jump shot from near the free-throw line with about 4:40 left on the second-half clock. Texas A&M counterattacked quickly, passing the ball down court to a streaking Ronnie Peret for what appeared to be an uncontested layup. Only Baylor's Tom Friedman had other ideas and showed a strong urge to not give up an easy basket despite the fact that the Bears already trailed 79–63. Five decades later, Sibley provided video and audio evidence of what happened next. One second Baylor radio broadcaster Frank Fallon was dutifully describing the closing minutes of a lopsided Texas A&M win, and then the next second he's trying to make sense of a melee: "Oh and Friedman . . . !" Fallon exclaimed, reacting to the foul, and then he abruptly switched gears. "Wait a minute. Now we've got a fight going on the floor. This is what we were afraid of. And we've got a fight going on the floor."

The broadcast, almost as if it's an old-time radio show, cuts in with a voice hollering, "Break it up! Break it up! Get out of there! Come on, Aggies! Break it up! Break it up! Break it up!"

Fallon lets us know that it's the voice of Coach Metcalf pleading with his people. The video, which is a little blurry, poorly lighted, and slightly grainy, starts a second or two after the hard foul. All that can really be seen is a flurry of punches, an unidentifiable player flying into the scrum, and ebbs and flows of humanity. Some seem to be attempting to break up the fight. Some clearly want more action. Metcalf, most likely using the arena's public address system, continues to implore the fans, "Come on, Aggies! Get back! Get back!"

Sibley recounted that it was one of the all-time hardest fouls that Friedman put on Peret. He described it as an error in calculation, considering members of the Texas A&M football team just happened to be sitting behind that goal. When fists started flying, Sibley saw red.

"A guy that's just an outlaw of a linebacker just beats Friedman to a pulp," Sibley said, but that wasn't his initial concern. "I wanted Barnett real bad. I went running in, and there was a cluster over Friedman, and I went in and shoved them away and tried to get to Barnett. Now it's like I'm in a hailstorm."

Sibley gave his account of the fight to the Associated Press for an article that ran in *The Bryan Daily Eagle* on February 20. "I was getting it pretty good around the head and shoulders," Sibley was quoted. "Stan Schlueter (another Baylor player) pulled one guy off me but somebody else hit me right here (behind the ear), and I went down right on top of Friedman. I got hit and kicked a lot then."

The same Thursday's *Fort Worth Star-Telegram* featured a centerpiece photo of a splayed-out Friedman on the front of the sports section. In the photo, Friedman's hands are raised above his head as he lays on the floor as if he might be unconscious. Baylor trainer David Hufstetler's hands can be seen as he administers aid to the fallen Bear.

On the radio broadcast, Fallon goes quiet for a few seconds after Metcalf's pleading with the combatants. The sound of the crowd roaring goes on, and then, forty-eight seconds into the audio clip and thirty-one seconds after the apparent beginning of the riot, the Texas A&M band strikes up the Star-Spangled Banner. In the video, bodies make an awkward, jerky transition from fighting, or attempting to break up the fight, to standing at attention (and some of them removing hats) for the national anthem.

That's how the riot ended.

Some accounts of the brawl claim that the Texas A&M Corps of Cadets rushed the court, but that isn't evident on the video, though only a portion of the court can be seen.

Bryan Daily Eagle sportswriter Jim Butler wrote a column placing the blame for the riot on game officials Percy Penn and Larry Covin, who he claimed let the physicality of the action get out of hand.

Sibley and Thompson each recalled trying to talk Menefee into taking the team and walking off the court instead of playing the final four and a half minutes. Meanwhile, Bowman remained calm and kept a low profile as the madness played out. He said his mother, Irene Barker, had come to the game. She was sitting behind the Baylor bench about halfway up the stands, and that gave him comfort.

"That was a pretty rough game for me. Rough from the standpoint that the fans were on me pretty good that game," Bowman said. "I didn't play very well that game. But when that brawl came, all I knew was my momma is in the stands, and I knew she was going to look after me. I wasn't that concerned about it."

Menefee told his players that they would finish the game. Texas A&M prevailed, 86–74, to gain a two-game lead on second-place Baylor. The Bears had won seven and lost three in SWC play to that point. The Aggies didn't open the door for a late charge in the final weeks of conference play. Texas A&M won the SWC title with a 12–2 league record, earning the automatic bid in the NCAA Tournament.

Baylor bounced back from the riot game to defeat SMU by twelve points in overtime in Dallas the following Saturday. Then the Bears dropped a home game by four points against TCU.

After wins over Arkansas and Texas Tech to finish the season, Baylor ended Bowman's junior season with an 18–6 overall record and a 10–4 mark in the SWC. That was the Bears' best finish since 1948, when they lost in the national championship game against Kentucky. Baylor finished second in conference. As mentioned before, there was not a conference tournament so the Bears had no shot at earning an NCAA bid that way. The season ended with a win in Lubbock. The Bears didn't go to the NCAA Tournament and were not invited to the sixteen-team National Invitational Tournament.

However, anyone looking for lingering resentment that Baylor didn't play under the bright lights of postseason basketball won't find it in Bowman.

"I think I was so elated and happy and blessed to be at Baylor, to be playing basketball at that level, and to be playing basketball well, I don't think anything could've happened to make me feel short-changed," he said.

Bowman was once again selected first-team All-SWC by both the United Press International and the *Waco Tribune-Herald*. He joined SMU's Gene Phillips and Bill Voight, Rice's Greg Williams, and Peret from Texas A&M on the UPI squad. The *Tribune-Herald* team selected the Aggies' Mike Heitman over SMU's Voight as a first-teamer but otherwise chose the same. Gatewood was second-team on both.

BAYLOR

1969-1970
PRESS GUIDE

Baylor seniors (from left) David Sibley, Tommy Bowman, and Larry Gatewood appear on the cover of the Baylor 1969–70 Press Guide along with head coach Bill Menefee (kneeling).

Courtesy of Baylor Athletics via the Texas Collection

13
Senior Season
Fall of 1969

As much as sports are part of the fabric of culture, sports are also sometimes perceived as being outside the definition of "real life." In whatever context we find it, sports are considered extracurricular. As such, when the very serious events of real life press in on us, it's hard to know what to do with sports.

In 1963, San Antonio Lee and San Antonio Brackenridge faced off in a high school football game so legendary it became known as "The Game" in the San Antonio area for decades. Part of its mystique is that it took place one week after President John F. Kennedy was assassinated in Dallas. Even as fans watched the game on regional television, they wondered how football would fit into such a surreal moment.

On September 14, 2001, high school football teams tiptoed back onto the field, leading the foray back into sports in the wake of the terrorist attacks that brought down the World Trade Center towers in New York City and shook the entire nation.

In the second half of 2020, the American sports world blindly wandered through seasons that were in constant peril of being suspended or ended because of virus outbreak during the COVID-19 pandemic.

The Baylor Bears basketball team began their 1969–70 campaign in such a moment. Baylor hosted Texas Wesleyan on

December 2, 1969, the day after the first draft lottery in the United States in twenty-seven years. The Vietnam War was escalating, and so was opposition to America's involvement. Even as the draft took place, at least one representative chosen to participate in the picking of numbers refused to take his turn, according to an Associated Press report. An article in the *Fort Worth Star-Telegram* described how anxious callers phoned the newsroom to learn the draft numbers of their birthdays as well as those for sons and boyfriends. The headline "News Room Gives Callers Heartache, Joy by the Number" may be among the most apt and accurate in the history of headline writing.

When Baylor and Texas Wesleyan tipped off for the Bears' season opener at eight p.m. at the Heart O' Texas Coliseum on December 2, it's likely every player on both teams knew his draft number. "The list drawn Monday night applied to all men between 19 and 26 years of age as of the end of this year," the AP article stated. Because freshmen were not eligible to play on the varsity, it's almost certain that the athletes in that game, and every college game that season, fell within that age range. Tommy Bowman had a high enough number that the prospect of being shipped to Southeast Asia to fight in an increasingly controversial war might have taken a back seat to playing his senior basketball season for the Bears. Married life might have also been on his mind. He and Jackie said their vows in May of that year. For the first time, he had his wife in the stands.

While Bowman and his teammates chased the same goals as the previous two seasons—wins that might ultimately result in a Southwest Conference title—his home life had leveled up. He no longer lived in a dorm and shared a room with David Sibley and David Croucher. By the fall of 1969, Bowman and Jackie lived in an apartment. Their home was close enough to Jackie's job at Region 12 Education Service Center for her to walk there if needed. With Tommy playing basketball and closing in on a degree from Baylor, it was Jackie's responsibility to bring home the rent money.

Bowman's senior season had another changing dimension about it. He had been a pioneer as Baylor's first African American scholarship athlete and the second Black player in the Southwest Conference. But that status was no longer singular and was becoming less unique. William Chatmon joined Baylor's roster from Tyler Junior College, giving the Bears two African American starters. Elsewhere in the SWC, Leroy Marion integrated Rice's varsity team that season. In a year, Gene Knolle would be Texas Tech's first Black varsity player, while Jimmy Blacklock integrated the University of Texas varsity.

The *Waco Tribune-Herald*'s season preview, now written by new beat writer Hollis Biddle, featured a photo of seniors David Sibley, Bowman, and Larry Gatewood standing shoulder-to-shoulder and leaning in over the head of a kneeling Bill Menefee. Biddle's article points out that the Bears had been picked to finish second in the SWC, not surprising since Baylor had ended up there in the previous two campaigns.

Baylor's season opened at home against Texas Wesleyan—not much of a challenge for this Bears team as they won, 89–49. Bowman scored the Bears' first points of the season just sixteen seconds into the contest. Then it was Chatmon jumping into the spotlight, though not in the most flattering way to start. The six-foot-six Chatmon was called for goaltending, which gave Texas Wesleyan its first points of the game. Even so, it was a nice debut for Chatmon by the end of the night. He and Bowman scored fourteen points apiece. Gatewood, as was his custom, led Baylor in scoring with fifteen.

The Bears had cruised to their first win, but that's all the ramp up they would get before facing much more serious early-season challenges. Four days after dismissing the Rams, Baylor traveled to Las Cruces, New Mexico, to face sixth-ranked New Mexico State (the game report added that New Mexico State was slotted at No. 2 in the country by *Sports Illustrated*). Baylor had risen to the top of the pack in the SWC and briefly entered the national rankings in February of 1969, but playing this New Mexico State team was something different. The Aggies roughed up Baylor, 102–83. New Mexico State guard Jimmy Collins scored twenty-three points, and center Sam Lacey added twenty-two and seventeen rebounds. In 1970, Lacey was picked fifth overall in the NBA draft by the Cincinnati Royals, and Collins was selected eleventh overall by the Chicago Bulls. New Mexico State, destined for the national semifinals later that season, thumped a Bears team that was still trying to figure out how its parts fit together.

Baylor continued on its westward trajectory and, two days later, played Arizona on the Wildcats' home court in Tucson. The Bears put up a better fight and went into halftime tied at forty. Bowman made a jumper just inside the free-throw line to pull Baylor within three points of Arizona in the final minute, but the Wildcats made the necessary free throws at the end to survive with an 81–76 victory over the Bears.

Under the radar, Menefee found something in Tucson that would bolster his team on the defensive end. Sophomore Tom Stanton spelled Bowman when the senior got in early foul trouble in both the first half and second half against the Wildcats.

"I was the last guy on the bench guarding the water bucket down there through the first three games of the season," Stanton said. "When I went in there at Las Cruces, I think I played the last ten or twelve minutes, and I just didn't do anything stupid. It wasn't like I did anything great. I didn't turn the ball over. I made a free throw, I think [versus Arizona]. Tommy picked up his second foul five minutes into the game. I'm down at the end of the bench. My roommate, Bob Griffitts, punched me and said, 'Coach Menefee wants you.' I looked up there, and he gave me the finger for me to come down to him. I pointed to myself like 'Me?' But he put me in to guard the guy that Tommy was guarding. I played the rest of the first half and went back to the bench in the second half. Tommy picked up his third foul about two minutes into the second half. Coach Menefee sent me in again. And again, I didn't do anything. I played good defense, and I think I scored two or three points."

Although Baylor had fallen to one win and two losses in the first week of the season, the trip out west showed the Bears had become more ambitious in their nonconference scheduling. The raised bar paid off in the near future.

Baylor evened its season record at home on December 11 by easing past Texas–Arlington. Chatmon had taken over the role of the Bears' go-to scorer and had twenty-five points and fifteen rebounds against the Rebels (UT–Arlington changed its nickname from Rebels to Mavericks in 1971). David Sibley had a double-double with twelve points and fourteen boards. Bowman hit just four of ten shots and had nine points, but he grabbed twelve rebounds to contribute to Baylor's 98–79 win at the Heart O' Texas Coliseum.

The UT-Arlington game was the first of a two-game home stand for Baylor. Southwestern Louisiana came to town two days later for what ended up being a bit of a revenge game. The Cajuns had beaten the Bears a year earlier when they shot forty-five free throws to Baylor's seventeen in Lafayette, Louisiana. But the Bears didn't need a parade to the free-throw line to turn the tables on Southwestern Louisiana. Chatmon took care of it. He scored thirty-six points, making fifteen of nineteen shot attempts from the field, and gathered in an amazing twenty-six rebounds. "Chatmon just had a sensational game," Menefee told Biddle.

Close behind, Gatewood scored thirty-two points as the duo almost outscored the Cajuns by themselves. Baylor prevailed, 95–68, despite the fact that Bowman got into foul trouble and had an uncharacteristically unproductive night.

With two home wins in their back pocket, the Bears had a 3–2 record as they headed to Abilene, Texas for the Cowboy Classic and opened the tournament with a 95–75 win over South Dakota. Bowman found his form again, scoring fifteen against the Coyotes. Chatmon did his thing with twenty-nine points and sixteen rebounds.

Under the radar, Stanton had become a more important piece in Baylor's game plan. He scored seven points against South Dakota, although his role was more concentrated on the defensive end. Stanton really made his presence felt the next night in a rematch with New Mexico State.

Baylor coach Bill Menefee instructs the Bears during a timeout.

Courtesy of Baylor Athletics via the Texas Collection

Exactly two weeks after the Aggies rolled up 102 points and beat Baylor by nineteen in Las Cruces, the two teams met again in Abilene. This time, New Mexico State came in ranked No. 3 in the nation. The *Tribune-Herald*'s game story about this go-round featured smiling mugs of Stanton and Bowman at the top of the sports page.

"Saturday's victory in the feature game of the Cowboy Classic will rank as one of the greatest of all time in Baylor basketball circles," claimed the *Tribune-Herald*'s game report. "The Bears probably have never beaten a more highly-ranked team in their entire history."

Although Baylor's basketball media almanac has New Mexico State ranked No. 13 instead of No. 3, it does confirm that the Bears' win over the Aggies was the highest-ranked opponent they had ever defeated at that time.

The game report credits Stanton, an Abilene native, for playing excellent defense on New Mexico State guard Collins, who still scored nineteen points. It also points out that Bowman moved inside on the defensive end and likely had a lot to do with holding Aggies star center Sam Lacey to fourteen.

Baylor led the rematch most of the way, but New Mexico State pulled even at sixty-two midway through the second half. And yet, the Bears didn't rattle. Stanton recalled: "We came out of the huddle (after a timeout), and Gatewood says, 'You know, Tom, we can beat these guys.' We beat them by twelve points in the last two minutes. It was a convincing win."

Baylor notched an 87–73 victory. The newspaper article called it Bowman's best game of the season as he had seventeen points. Chatmon, of course, led the Bears with twenty-six, and Gatewood added twenty. Stanton scored nine, and his defensive contributions were duly recognized.

Alas, the high of the win over a ranked team might have worked against Baylor. After beating New Mexico State on Saturday, December 20, the Bears went to Shreveport, Louisiana and lost to Centenary, 78–74, the following Monday.

"We're getting ready to break into the top twenty-five, and we go to Centenary and lose," Sibley said. "I thought [assistant coach Carroll Dawson] was going to commit suicide."

That's how Baylor went into Christmas break in 1969. The Bears came back from the holiday and played Centenary again at the HOT Coliseum on December 30. This time, they won, 86–60. Chatmon and Gatewood combined for thirty points in the first half as the Bears cruised to a fifteen-point lead at the break. Biddle noted that Bowman once again showed flashes of brilliance as he contributed ten points and nine rebounds.

Three days later, Baylor finished its nonconference schedule by hosting undefeated Wyoming. The Baylor media almanac doesn't list Wyoming as a ranked opponent, but Biddle's game story states that the Cowboys were slotted at No. 14 nationally. Baylor posted an 86–79 triumph over Wyoming as four players scored in double digits. Gatewood led the way with twenty-five, Tom Friedman had twenty-two, Chatmon scored seventeen with twenty-one rebounds, and Bowman pitched in sixteen points and nine boards. Menefee pointed out that Jerry Hopkins played well. That meant the Bears had a couple of all-conference types in Gatewood and Bowman plus a new prolific scorer and rebounder in Chatmon and quality role players with Friedman, Stanton, and Hopkins. Even with Sibley fighting through some small, nagging injuries and playing fewer minutes, Baylor had a lot of momentum going into Southwest Conference action.

But the Bears didn't make it into the top twenty-five either following the New Mexico State triumph or for the remainder of the campaign despite building up a record of 11–3 near the end of January.

Baylor was set to open SWC play at home against preseason conference favorite Texas on January 5, and tickets were selling fast. The Bears had won six of seven as Bowman, Gatewood, Sibley, and company came down the home stretch of their college careers.

(WAC~L (WACO TEXAS JAN 24 BAYLOR WINS 3 RD CONFRENCE GAME
Baylor forward Tommy Bowman comes down with one of Baylor's
40 rebounds early in tonights 110 to 76 victory over the
Arkansas Razorbacks. Baylors 110 points is a team scoring
record and the most points scored against the Razorbacks in
a conference game.
AP WIREPHOYO str jw

Courtesy of the Texas Sports Hall of Fame. Photo by Jimmy Willis.

14
Senior Season
SWC Play, 1970

Several times during Tommy Bowman's Baylor career, with his friends David Sibley, David Croucher, and Larry Gatewood joining him, the Bears reached the brink of college basketball greatness. They were right there. In the three years that Bowman and company led the Baylor varsity, their team defeated opponents that went on to win games in the (then much more exclusive) NCAA Tournament. They established themselves as legitimate contenders for the Southwest Conference title and played in games in 1968 and 1969 that more or less decided the conference championship.

As SWC play tipped off in 1970, Baylor had reached that point again. The Bears had beaten ranked opponents in nonconference play—No. 3 New Mexico State and No. 14 Wyoming. They began conference with a 7–3 record and might have been in the national top twenty-five if not for an unsightly loss at Centenary.

With a hindsight view of Bowman's era at Baylor, arguments can be made for all of his Bears teams being the best of the time, the closest to breaking through to an SWC title and the NCAA Tournament. Obviously, the 1968 Baylor squad that played TCU at the Heart O' Texas Coliseum in the final game of the season with the conference championship at stake came the closest on paper. That team was led by sophomores and might have won the SWC going away if it had not been for nagging injuries suffered by seniors Russell Kibbe and Ed Thorpe. The Bears' 1969 team won the most games of the three, finishing with an 18–6 mark and 10–4 in conference. That team was a little deeper too, with Tom Friedman, Eddie Frazier, and Randy Thompson playing key roles and Richard Scallorn, Steve Bartels, and Stan Schlueter all serving as members of the supporting cast. The 1969 group earned a No. 19 national ranking, the only time the Bears were ranked for a fifty-nine-year period from 1949 to 2008 (according to Baylor's media almanac).

Bowman himself is reluctant to look back at his college basketball career with much of a measuring stick. He has stated time and time again that he was blessed by God to be playing college basketball at that level. However, as he and Tom Stanton drove home from a team gathering in Huntsville in the summer of 2022, he offered some analysis.

"On the way back the other day I asked Tommy, 'You played on three Baylor teams—which one was best?'" Stanton revealed, "Tommy said, 'There's no doubt which one was best. That was our team.'"

Bowman gave as evidence the 1969–70 team's depth of seniors with Gatewood, Sibley, Croucher, and himself, combined with the soaring junior college transfer Chatmon and a talented group of sophomores. Stanton and Pat Fees had both earned high school All-American honors and came to Baylor with a healthy dose of hype.

The Bears' 1969–70 team showed signs of having a high ceiling as it thumped Texas, 81–59, to start the SWC on January 5, 1970 in Waco. *Tribune-Herald* beat writer Hollis Biddle heaped praises on Baylor's cagers as they had vaulted into the new year. He noted early in his game story that Texas was picked as the conference favorite and went on endorsing the squad. "Menefee's Bears came to play. They were ready above and beyond the call of duty. Ready mentally and physically. And 7,500 fans cheered them to the rafters. . . . The Bears clicked as a team, excelled individually and took the boys in the fancy pants apart, piece by piece."

Bowman had eleven rebounds and, though he only scored nine points, excelled at finding Chatmon open for easy baskets. Gatewood led Baylor in scoring with twenty-four. When Chatmon, who finished with sixteen, got into foul trouble midway through the second half and went to the bench with the Bears' lead at eight points, Gatewood responded with a pair of crucial buckets that pushed the advantage back to a dozen. Baylor easily won the closing minutes to start SWC action with a big confidence boost.

The Texas game fell on a Monday night, long before the days of ESPN's Big Monday, but the effect was similar. Baylor posted a big win early in the week and then had a wealth of time to prepare to travel to Texas A&M on Saturday. The roll continued as the Bears avenged the 1969 riot game with a 79–71 victory over the Aggies. Gatewood, still feeling the hot hand, poured in thirty-one points, the most a Baylor player had ever scored against Texas A&M to that point in the rivalry, which dated to 1915. Bowman had a quiet contest, though the *Tribune-Herald* reported that he grabbed a key rebound with 1:37 left and the Bears ahead by four. Sibley made his presence felt once again as he scored five consecutive points when he got in the game in the second half. He finished with nine and added three rebounds. Croucher also contributed a basket and some vital minutes off the bench.

That's how Baylor went into the break for fall semester final exams. The Bears had two weeks before resuming SWC play versus Arkansas. In that time, they could boast about a 9–3 record and a place atop the conference standings at 2–0.

In each of the previous two seasons, Baylor brought in Tarleton State to help restart the engines following semester exams. The Bears didn't have that luxury in 1970 as they came back from break with a home game against the Razorbacks. But at least it was a well-below-average Arkansas team that brought a 2–10 record to town.

Baylor didn't mess around. The Bears took the first half to figure out the Hogs' zone defense and then exploded for one of the most spectacular twenty minutes in program history. "The second half was amazing," Menefee told Biddle. "I just can't explain it." Menefee watched his team light up the scoreboard for seventy-one points to close out a 110–76 triumph over struggling Arkansas. Biddle wrote that it was Bowman's best game of the season as he scored twenty points and hauled in seventeen rebounds. He and Chatmon (twenty-one points, seventeen boards) couldn't be stopped or blocked out in the lane.

It was a night for everyone to get into the act. Gatewood had a cool twenty-four points. Tom Friedman scored eighteen with nine rebounds, and Pat Fees came off the bench for sixteen points and six boards. Sibley, still recovering from a back injury and surrendering minutes to the prolific Chatmon, added four points. Jerry Hopkins made a basket and a free throw for three points. Stanton was just about the only player to produce less than his average as he made just one of seven shots and had two points. Keith Curlee made an appearance and connected on the only shot he took.

Of course, one of the things that makes sports so dramatic, so entertaining, and yet so maddening is sheer unpredictability. Three days after its display of prolific offense against the Razorbacks, on the same home court where the Bears seemingly couldn't miss, Baylor found itself grinding out a slugfest with Texas Tech.

Chatmon proved the hero as he rebounded a Texas Tech missed free throw with eighteen seconds left in the second half and the Red Raiders ahead by a point. Chatmon passed the ball out to Friedman and darted down the court. With nine seconds left, Hopkins got the ball back to Chatmon under the basket, and he banked in a shot around Texas Tech's Jerry Turner for the win.

Baylor prevailed, 47–46, and held on to first place in the SWC standings through four games. Bowman produced a double-double against the Red Raiders with twelve points and twelve rebounds, and the newspaper article featured a large photo of him driving to the basket for a layup. Chatmon's game-winner was one of the few times he solved the Texas Tech defense as he finished with just six points.

It's been stated before in this story, but it bears repeating as the Baylor basketball team held a lead in the conference standings: the margin for error for making it to postseason basketball from the SWC in the late 1960s and early 1970s was razor thin. With no conference tournament to earn an automatic bid and the NCAA Tournament taking in the ballpark of twenty-four teams, winning the SWC title was the only way to make it. That meant outlasting a double round robin with eight other schools with the utmost of familiarity with each other. Not until Houston joined the league and dominated with its Phi Slama Jama dynasty and Arkansas followed suit under Nolan Richardson was there an annual odds-on favorite, and by then March Madness had expanded and the SWC hosted a postseason tourney.

The 4–0 Bears hit their first bump in pursuit of the elusive SWC title in Fort Worth on January 31. Baylor couldn't slow down TCU the whole game and, after the Bears jumped ahead 11–1 in the early running, couldn't keep up with the Horned Frogs either. TCU's six-foot-eight forward Doug Boyd set a TCU record with twenty-seven rebounds, single-handedly keeping Baylor from many second chances on the offensive end. But the Bears would have needed a lot of them anyway. TCU won, 90–71, and handed Baylor its first SWC loss of the season.

Baylor needed a second half rally the following Tuesday to force overtime against SMU. But the Bears won the extra period and claimed an 83–81 win that kept them tied with TCU for first place in the SWC table. Gatewood was a perfect nine-for-nine from the free-throw line against the Mustangs and led Baylor with twenty-nine points. His final two free throws gave the Bears a four-point lead with five seconds left in OT. Bowman fouled out late in regulation and missed the extra period, but he contributed fifteen points and eight rebounds.

Throughout its seventy-plus-year history, Rice's Autry Court, now called Tudor Fieldhouse, hasn't exactly been a lair of doom for visiting basketball teams. However, in early February of 1970, hoops was a hot topic on the Owls' campus. Rice had an 8–8 overall record, but the Owls were close behind TCU and Baylor in the SWC race at 4–2 as they hosted Baylor on February 7. Rice had a good night as Tom Myer pumped in twenty-one points and Gary Reist added fifteen.

But it also coincided with a poor shooting half for Baylor down the stretch. The Bears connected on just eight field goals in the second half. Rice led 71–67 with a minute and a half to play. Although the Owls scored just one point in the final one hundred seconds, Baylor still could not overtake the home team and fell, 72–71. Gatewood attempted a half-court shot at the buzzer that came up short.

Maybe a one-point loss on the road against a decent Rice team didn't hurt too bad. It stung worse when the Bears dropped a 76–75 decision at Arkansas the following Saturday. Baylor had drubbed the Hogs by thirty-one just a couple of weeks earlier at the HOT Coliseum. A much different game developed in Fayetteville and one that Bowman may have mercifully forgotten.

With eight seconds left in the second half and the game tied at 75, Baylor ran a play designed to win it. But Chatmon's shot with five seconds to go missed, and Arkansas got the ball to senior forward Robert McKenzie near mid-court. McKenzie heaved a desperation shot that missed. In accordance with one of the unwritten rules of basketball—that the refs shouldn't decide the game by calling a shooting foul at half court with time running out—the Razorbacks and Bears should've headed to overtime. But the ref blew his whistle and called Bowman for a foul.

Bowman recollects an instant on the court when he told the official, "Ref, I didn't even touch that guy, and I'm as sure of that as I am being Black." And then Bowman also remembers what happened next. "BEEP! [Bowman makes a T sign with his hands] He shot me with a technical. That's the only tech I ever got. He read more into it. I was just telling him I was sure I didn't touch the guy." This instant might have happened on that night in Fayetteville. Stanton remembered the closing seconds of that game and said Bowman was nowhere near McKenzie.

Nevertheless, with no time left on the clock, McKenzie stepped to the free-throw line and buried his first shot, giving Arkansas the victory to the delight of the Barnhill Field House crowd. The game story doesn't mention a technical foul on Bowman, but it wouldn't have mattered anyway as McKenzie's first free throw decided the outcome.

Baylor's losses in conference were starting to get typecast, and the Bears' next installment enforced the trend. Rice came to Waco eight days after the Owls' narrow victory at Autry Court for a Saturday game at the HOT Coliseum. With Myer and Reist leading the way, Rice surged ahead in the second half. The Owls held on to a three- or four-point lead for most of the final ten minutes, but they opened the door by failing to score in the game's last two minutes.

Alas, Baylor couldn't walk through. The Bears drew a couple of charging calls on the defensive end, then failed to convert them into baskets on offense until Gatewood connected with twelve seconds remaining. Rice escaped with a 61–60 victory.

"They now have the patent on one-point defeats," Biddle wrote about the Bears in his game story.

Baylor could have maintained a share of the SWC lead with a home win over Rice. Instead, the Owls moved to the top of the standings by themselves. The Bears were fading out of contention as they were two games behind Rice in the standings and in a pack that included TCU, Texas Tech, and Texas A&M in close pursuit.

SMU gave Baylor another gut-punch in a Tuesday night game in Dallas. The seventh-place Mustangs protected their home court, 70–66, and all but doomed the Bears' chances for a conference championship. Baylor had lost four straight games, and its combined margin of defeat was seven points.

Stanton still thinks about all the close losses that separated Baylor from a run at the SWC title in 1970. It's something he and Bowman have talked about too, including on their ride home from Huntsville.

"You know, Mad Dog, we should've won the conference by two or three games easily," Bowman told Stanton.

"And he's right," Stanton said. "Some try to forget it. I've never been able to forget it."

After Rice finished off a season sweep of the Bears, the Owls had opened up a two-game lead in the conference standings. Rice finished the job and earned the SWC berth in the NCAA Tournament. As of this publication, fifty-three years later, that stands as the Owls' last trip to the Big Dance.

Baylor fell to fifth, three games out with four remaining on the schedule. The Bears bounced back on the weekend with a 92–81 wound-licking win over TCU. The game article in the *Tribune-Herald* once again featured a large action shot of Bowman jumping to make a pass. He scored thirteen points with thirteen rebounds. Chatmon scored thirty-two points and matched Bowman on the boards as the two players formed the muscle in Baylor's flex.

After an 81–70 loss at Texas, the Bears returned home for the final home game for Bowman, Gatewood, Sibley, and Croucher, all of whom had been in the program together since their freshman season. Baylor hosted Texas A&M. It must have been satisfying for the Bears players, in particular those who played in the 1969 riot game in College Station, to read the headline "Bears Snip Aggie Title Run, 70–68." All four seniors played significant roles in the win as mentioned in Biddle's game story: "Bruin seniors Tommy Bowman and Larry Gatewood closed out their Heart O' Texas careers with 10 and 11 points respectively. . . . Menefee also got another good bench performance from David Croucher, Jerry Hopkins, and David Sibley."

There was some talk, as Baylor traveled to Lubbock for the regular season finale, that the National Invitational Tournament had its eyes on the Bears. A motivated Baylor team defeated Texas Tech, 80–72. Biddle wrote that it was one of Bowman's best games of the season as he scored twenty points and pulled in fourteen rebounds. Stanton poured in fifteen in the first half to help the Bears take control of the contest.

But there was no NIT bid. As in the previous two seasons, the last game on the schedule was the last game. It lacked the type of ending that it deserved. Chatmon replaced Bowman on the All-Conference first teams, though Bowman received honorable mention on the UPI's All-SWC squad.

Three and a half years after Bowman walked into a gym at Baylor wondering if he could compete at the major college level, he had established himself as one of the great ones. Decades later he entered the SWC Hall of Fame. A photo of Bowman going up for a dunk can be seen at the Texas Sports Hall of Fame building on University Parks Drive in Waco, where the SWC Hall has its home.

But the stats, the awards, the honors, the place in history—they're all second fiddle to the kid from Athens, Texas.

"Some of the best relationships that God placed in my life were from Baylor University," Bowman said. "I'll tell anybody. I value the academics. I value the diploma. I value the things that have happened to me through Baylor University. But the most important thing I got from Baylor was the relationships. I spoke to a group of kids awhile back and that's what I told them. Get all you can from your instructors, professors. But at some point in time you're going to realize the most valuable thing you'll receive is relationships. I think that's the most important thing in my life."

Tommy Bowman's graduation photo.

Courtesy of the Bowman Family

15
Graduation

The Baylor campus has changed so much in the last fifty years that it's practically been reinvented since the late 1960s and early 1970s when Tommy Bowman walked across it. That's nothing spectacular. Waco has changed in that time as well. Baylor and Waco exist as parallel and symbiotic entities in Central Texas. Their fates are tied. Both have weathered the storms of scandals that made national news. But in the 2010s and 2020s both ascended the rollercoaster hill. Chip and Joanna Gaines have created the *Fixer Upper* universe, and tourists now flock to Waco to shop in grain silos and visit remodeled 1960s-era houses. Kim Mulkey built a women's basketball powerhouse that helped Baylor make it through dark days on the football field and within the men's basketball program. Then Scott Drew's Baylor Bears emerged as a national power.

Like everywhere else, technology transformed academic life at Baylor. Actually sitting in a classroom as a professor lectures isn't yet a quaint, throwback experience, but it's getting there. Students had the ability to take a class online or to get a credit without ever writing on paper with a pen before the onset of the COVID-19 pandemic. Then the coronavirus accelerated the remote learning train. It's still a challenge for a student athlete to compete at an extraordinary level while keeping up with schoolwork and staying on track for a diploma. But a Baylor basketball player now has access to everything he or she needs to participate in lectures or do homework via the internet on the airplane to road games, in the hotel on game day, and everywhere in between until he or she can get back through the doors of the academic halls (and even walking to those academic halls while in town might not be completely necessary).

All of that contrasts with the Baylor University that Tommy Bowman attended as he finished up his business degree during the 1970–71 school year.

Bowman very much lived in the world of trudging to professors' offices to obtain makeup material before or after frequent road trips during the fall and spring semesters of his playing career. He typed his papers on a typewriter (Jackie remembers times when she and a friend volunteered as typists). College life a half century ago was analog.

So Bowman needed a fifth year of college to finish, as many student athletes did at the time. But he got there with little fanfare in the spring of 1971.

"My mom thought he hung the moon. When he graduated Baylor, she was very, very proud of him and so was I," Jackie Bowman said.

The fifth year also gave Bowman a chance to see his influence firsthand. William Chatmon and Tom Stanton returned to lead the Bears in 1970–71 and were joined by a talented guard and forward named Roy Thomas. Chatmon and Thomas had previously played together at Tyler Junior College during Thomas's freshman season. He said he was one letter grade in a history class away from being able to transfer after one year and join Chatmon on the team with Bowman, Sibley, Croucher, and the other 1969–70 seniors. Instead, Thomas came to Baylor as a junior in the fall of 1970 and quickly befriended Bowman, who was a common presence around the Bears team.

At the time, Thomas appreciated Bowman as an experienced college student and a friendly face as the younger man navigated life on a white-dominated campus. Thomas made frequent trips to the Bowmans' apartment, where he enjoyed friendship and hospitality.

After finishing his college career at Baylor and briefly playing pro basketball in Europe, Thomas joined Jim Haller's coaching staff and played a key role in recruiting Vinnie Johnson and Terry Teagle to the Bears. Thus forms the direct link between Bowman and two of Baylor basketball's top NBA success stories. The connection isn't lost on Thomas after all these decades. He said Bowman had the perfect temperament to become Baylor's first Black scholarship athlete because, whatever he faced, Bowman didn't carry bitterness with him. That personality trait, maybe more than any other factor, allowed Bowman to pave the way for all the African American men and women who followed him into the Baylor basketball programs.

Tommy and Jackie Bowman have lived most of their lives in a home just a few miles from the Baylor campus. In one way or another, they've stayed connected to the school. They had plenty of photos to offer for this project—Tommy posed with his teammates at reunions, candid shots from occasions when he has been recognized for his contributions to Baylor. But one lasting image has been lost in physical form. It still means a lot to Jackie Bowman, and it symbolizes what Bowman and Baylor meant to each other.

"I've got this picture in my mind when he made a gesture to the crowd, like 'Hooray we did it,'" she said. "A fist pump up to the crowd, and the crowd responded. I thought that was just outstanding for the crowd to respond to him that way."

Tommy and Jackie Bowman pose with their grandchildren (from left) Tyler
Bowman, Mason Agbahiwe and Emery Agbahiwe.

Photo by Sylvester Agbahiwe

16
Life after Basketball

Although it's been more than fifty years since Tommy Bowman played basketball for Baylor, some things in his life haven't changed much since then. He and his wife, Jackie, were married between Bowman's junior and senior years of college, and now they've walked through life together for over half a century. Their son, Tommy Bowman II, was born in 1972, followed by their daughter, Krystal (now Krystal Agbahiwe) in 1981. Both Tommy II and Krystal grew up in the same house in East Waco, and that's where Tommy and Jackie continue to live.

Over and over, in interviews for this book and every time Bowman speaks publicly or is interviewed, he gives God the glory for his being chosen to play basketball at Baylor and, in doing so, becoming the school's first Black scholarship athlete.

That's how Bowman views his post-Baylor-basketball life as well.

"I just never dreamed . . . I've had two jobs since I graduated from Baylor," Bowman said, marveling at the trajectory of his own professional life. "I worked for Central Freight for thirty-two years. And I've worked (at Lipsitz in Waco), May (of 2022) will be eighteen years. I got jobs at both these places without filling out an application. That's God. That doesn't have anything to do with me. That was God."

Bowman graduated from Baylor in the spring of 1971. He was not selected in the 1970 NBA Draft, nor were Larry Gatewood or David

Sibley. In fact, according to basketball-reference.com, there were no Southwest Conference players drafted in the first one hundred picks. However, there were four Stephen F. Austin players drafted in that less-than-exclusive group and another from Paul Quinn College in Waco. TCU's Doug Boyd was the first SWC player taken in the 1970 draft in the eighth round with the 127th pick.

Before Bowman's Baylor career ended, there had been a suggestion that he could tour with the Harlem Globetrotters. Tommy II saw a clip of a newspaper article describing how Globetrotter advance man Bobby Milton had his eyes on the Bears' star. The younger Tommy Bowman was well into his forties when he read the newspaper clipping, which was in a box of memorabilia that Jackie had kept.

"If there's a picture of a person in the dictionary by humble, it'd probably be him," Tommy II said. "That's just who he is. You would never know that he did any of this. I'm learning stuff as we go. That's how much he didn't really talk about it."

Bowman didn't sign on with the Harlem Globetrotters. He did spend a couple of days at a training camp in New Orleans, presumably with the New Orleans Buccaneers of the American Basketball Association.

"I was invited to come down and try out in New Orleans. I think I stayed three or four days," Bowman said. "I decided I needed to go back to Waco. After practice one day, I just put my stuff in my car and came back here."

Tommy and Jackie were still living in a second-story apartment near Baylor. Jackie said she assumed Tommy would draw from his reserves of mental toughness and do whatever it took to make the New Orleans club. Looking back, she realizes that God had another calling for her husband.

"One evening I heard his footsteps coming up the stairs," Jackie said. "I asked him, 'What are you doing here so early?' He started to tell me some things they had to do. The Lord had different ideas."

Bowman went to work at Central Freight right out of college. Speaking with family members, it's clear he has an inherited work ethic. His aunt, Lynda Pierce, talks about how her father, Bowman's grandfather, Gaston Bowman, worked seven days a week to provide for the family.

But there's also an element of Tommy Bowman's personality that he seems to have gleaned from his time at Baylor. He came out of college a more assertive person than the young man who essentially followed his mother's intentions and signed on with Carroll Dawson and Bill Menefee's Baylor program.

The more mature, outgoing Bowman is evident in the story of his first interaction with a fellow Central Freight employee named Gary Thomas, who would become a longtime close friend.

"There I was, transferred from Dallas to Waco to the corporate headquarters. He didn't know me from Adam, and yet he invited me on the first day to his home for supper," Thomas recalled. "I was very impressed by that. He and Jackie, his wife, they were just so kind and cordial. I was really impacted by his kindness and his Christian manner."

Thomas started out working on the docks at Central Freight when he was in high school. He put himself through college in that job and continued with the company after he earned his degree. When Thomas came to Waco, Bowman's role was managing worker's compensation claims. The two men were not in the same department but became close nonetheless.

They bonded in a unique partnership outside of their daily activities. In those days, before Central Freight was sold to an out-of-state company, it owned and maintained a 5,500-acre deer camp near Fredericksburg, Texas. Thomas said that dock workers, drivers, and shop personnel who had stayed injury-free for a year were invited to spend a weekend hunting or even just relaxing at the camp. Thomas and Bowman traveled together to run the camp most weekends during the fall. They prepared and served meals, did the cleaning, and generally acted as hosts on Central Freight's behalf.

"During the time that we had free, when we weren't taking out hunters or picking up hunters or preparing meals, we had some time to just sit around and visit," Thomas said. "In those quiet moments out in the woods, we had time to talk about our lives. I learned about his love for his family and how much his dear grandmother was an influence on his life as a young child and as a teenager. That sort of solidified his character and his personality. I've never met a man that I have more respect for than Tommy. In hard circumstances, he would rely on his grandmother's words."

Thomas played a key part in the impetus for this biography along with Sibley. By the time the project started, Thomas had learned that he had an aggressive and life-threatening form of cancer. He died on September 10, 2022. But he was able to offer his perspective on his friend's internal motivation.

"What he said is what he did. What he believed is what his standard in life was," Thomas said. "He's a Bible-studying Christian, and he makes those applications to scripture in his daily life. He's honest, he's forthright. He's aboveboard. He has no agenda that he's riding behind. He's just a good, honest, down-to-earth, sincere individual."

Another close friend at Central Freight, Lee McKnight, recalled how well Bowman handled difficult situations. McKnight managed the line department and the dispatching of trucks. That's where Bowman came to work and where they met. McKnight confirmed that truck drivers can be a rough crowd, but they weren't going to walk over Bowman.

McKnight told the story of one particular driver who was prone to griping about his assignments. No matter the route, he had some sort of complaint. One day he picked up his marching orders at the dispatching station and, as usual, didn't like it. As he walked away, he audibly mumbled a curse and a slur directed at Bowman. The six-foot-four former All-Southwest Conference forward quickly came out of the office to further discuss the matter, but the line driver scurried away.

"There was no licks hit, no fistfights or anything like that," McKnight said. "He was a guy that was hard to dispatch to start with. Ultimately, I fired the guy."

Bowman had the toughness and restraint to last.

"I had him on the evening shift and the graveyard shift from 11 at night until 7 the next day," McKnight said. "That's the time when all the line drivers are winding up their nights' work. Naturally, they're not in a good mood (laughing). Tommy handled it quite well. As a matter of fact, he became quite well liked by the line drivers. He was that kind of personality. I never heard Tommy use a swear word in all the time we were together."

Bowman continued with Central Freight until the mid-1990s. He, Jackie, and Krystal moved to Arkansas briefly around 1997 when he went to work for Wal-Mart. They kept their house, in which Tommy II lived while attending McLennan Community College. And then the Bowman family returned after a year away. Krystal started her junior year of high school at Waco High, and Tommy picked back up with Central Freight.

He stayed at the job for as long as he could tolerate the new ownership. Then Bowman transitioned to Lipsitz and remained there until his retirement at the end of 2022.

Tom Stanton helped connect Bowman with Tommy Salome, who is credited with making Lipsitz a leader in the scrap recycling industry in Texas.

"Tommy told me that when he went to work for Tommy Salome, there were like four trucks and they've got a fleet of thirty-five or forty now," Stanton said. "Tommy (Bowman) was the guy with the character that helped develop all that."

Bowman stayed around basketball, playing in rec leagues and pick-up games at the Bledsoe-Miller gymnasium on Martin Luther King Boulevard in Waco, near his home. He also stayed connected with Baylor, including serving as a member of the school's board of regents.

Tommy Bowman II watched his father play basketball in various settings growing up. The younger Tommy Bowman also knew from an early age that his father had been Baylor's first Black scholarship athlete. But that distinction didn't completely settle in until well into the twenty-first century. Tommy II said it was during a ceremony for his father and teammates during a Big 12 basketball game that his father's role really gripped him.

"That was maybe 2016, 2017," Tommy II said. "I started putting dates with it–1966 wasn't that long ago. I was born in '72. It made more of an impact in my life. So now it means more to me."

Tommy II lives in the Dallas/Fort Worth suburb of Euless and, like his father, works in the trucking business as a trailer mechanic. He played high school basketball at Waco High and has stayed involved in the game as a coach of his son's team's traveling club.

The Bowman family can easily trace their basketball lineage. Although Tommy II said his father stressed academics more than sports, there was a time to teach hoops as well.

"The first thing he talked about was form," Tommy II said. "This is how you should hold the basketball and shoot it. This is what you want to do. I could see him reminisce and just the joy it brought to him to be able to sit there and say, 'Do this and this.'"

One of Tommy II's thrills is to have his dad come to his son Tyler's games.

"Anything basketball, if I got his approval, I was cool," Tommy II said. "I still do that, matter of fact. We took some teams to San Antonio, and I had coached one by myself. To have him sitting there, selfishly, I'm like, 'Come watch your grandson.' But really I'm like, 'Come watch me get to coach these kids.' We won, but I was more concerned with, 'Hey, what did you think?'"

It is a struggle for Tommy II and Krystal to tempt their mom and dad out of Waco. Tommy Bowman admits he doesn't like to travel much. That might be an inclination of his personality, but it's probably influenced as well by his dedication to his church. Tommy and Jackie attend Toliver Chapel Missionary Baptist Church in Waco, where Tommy serves as chairman of deacons.

Krystal said a typical interaction would be for her to suggest to her parents that they come to Houston for a birthday party or a similar social event only to hear her father say that he can't be away from church on Sunday because he needs to oversee Communion. She knows her dad hates driving in big cities. The chance to see her kids, Mason and Emery, Tommy and Jackie's grandchildren, are Krystal's best bet to get her parents to make the trip. Even so, her father's dedication to serve in the church is genuine.

Krystal had a memorable conversation with her eight-year-old son, Mason, about advice that Mason had gleaned from LeBron James. From a LeBron interview, Mason had learned that a person needs to work hard to earn the chance to win. Krystal was curious what advice her dad would give Mason.

"So, we called my dad and he said, 'I want you to always remember to keep Christ the focus of your life.' I was like, 'Well, Daddy, is that what you want to tell him?'" Krystal said. "But if he didn't say something about Christ, he wouldn't be being true to himself. First and foremost, he is a Christian. After that he's a husband, a father, he's a grandfather, he's a brother, and it all comes in line."

Dr. Jimmy D. Hunter is the pastor at Toliver Chapel Missionary Baptist. He said he has been particularly blessed by his partnership with Bowman as the church's chairman of deacons. Dr. Hunter has seen how Bowman's humble spirit serves him well as a leader.

In turn, Dr. Hunter has seized the opportunity to hold up Bowman as an example to others.

"After he was inducted into the Southwest Conference Hall of Fame, I had (a picture of) his banner blown up and put in a very large frame," Dr. Hunter said. "The Sunday that (the Baylor Religious Hour choir) came for college day, I presented that picture to him along with a trophy of a basketball player. I kind of created some hype because I wanted them to know he was the first African American basketball player at Baylor."

Dr. Hunter can be counted among the group of people who would like to see Baylor put more of a spotlight on Bowman's success at the school, particularly with a statue at the basketball facility.

Tommy II has seen up close how his father reacts with surprise when he is brought forward by the Bears basketball program. On the same night that Bowman was recognized during a Big 12 game and

Tommy Bowman serves as the chairman of deacons at Toliver Chapel
Missionary Baptist Church in Waco.

Photograph by Sylvester Agbahiwe

the ceremony changed Tommy II's perspective, the older Bowman
was surprised when some of the Kansas State contingent sought him
out to have pictures taken with him.

Similarly, the Baylor team that won the 2021 national championship honored Bowman.

"He pretty much said it, and you could hear it in his voice, that
he's shocked that those guys wanted to honor him with a jersey,"
Tommy II said. "He kept expressing to me, 'Hey, they actually know
who I am.'"

As a young man, Bowman felt the pressures of being thrust into
a pioneering role. He doesn't put it that way, but the stories about
him reveal that's what happened. Baylor assistant coach Carroll
Dawson signed Bowman because Dawson saw in him the qualities
needed to be the school's first Black scholarship athlete.

Bowman excelled in that role, but he wasn't any kind of wall-
flower. Most of his teammates have stories about altercations with
him on the court, when the competitiveness of the moment brought

out his aggressive side. Looking back, Bowman is still a little baffled by those moments.

"I can remember Jerry Hopkins when he was a transfer from junior college. I feel so ashamed," Bowman said. "We got into a situation where he and I were in a heated argument. He just said, 'If you want to hit me, go ahead and hit me.' He walked up to me with hands down to his sides. I just popped him. I never had a guy walk up in my face and say, 'Go ahead and hit me. Hit me!' So I hit him."

As Hopkins sat drinking iced tea in Huntsville, Texas, in the summer of 2022, he remembered that incident as an anomaly. More recently, Hopkins has become much more acquainted with Bowman's compassionate side.

"The day after my wife passed five years ago, Tommy called me," Hopkins said. "We hadn't spoken in a year. After that, he would call me every two or three days or text me a scripture."

That's the life that Bowman is striving for.

"My prayer every morning is that at the end of the day I treat everybody—everybody, not just the drivers (at work), not just the customers, everybody I come in contact with—with dignity and with respect," Bowman said. "No matter how they treat me. That's how I was raised up."

Tommy Bowman and Tommy Bowman II pose together at the Athens High
School Athletics Hall of Fame inaugural induction ceremony in
December 2022.

Photo by Chad Conine

Epilogue

It's too easy to write that Tommy Bowman's life came full circle on the night of December 8, 2022. That's the evening he joined the inaugural class of Athens ISD's Athletic Hall of Fame as they were inducted with a dinner ceremony at Athens Country Club.

When Bowman's name is mentioned in Waco, Texas, or among alumni of Baylor University, much of the time, it is probably because he was the first Black scholarship athlete at Baylor and the first African American member of the Bears' basketball program. Certainly, he was great on the court. Sophomore of the year honors and an All-Southwest Conference performance all three years of his varsity career attest to that. His inductions into the Baylor Athletics Hall of Fame in 1999 and the SWC Hall of Fame in 2018 count as further evidence.

But on most days of his life in the last fifty-plus years, Bowman has been a husband, a father, an employee, a manager, a deacon, and a friend. As his daughter, Krystal Agbahiwe, stressed, he has striven to be a follower of Jesus Christ above all. The ability to shoot a basketball or block out an opponent for a rebound hasn't been a factor in any of those pursuits. Bowman's length and quickness that made him a top-notch defender on the court didn't translate into the offices of Central Freight or Lipsitz. The hoops skills don't make him a better deacon. In fact, it's more accurate to say that his core beliefs, along with helping him navigate work and family life all these years, were present and valuable when he served as a pioneer in the SWC of the 1960s.

Even so, there was something special about Bowman entering the Athens Sports Hall. It wasn't just that he returned to a place where he had also been a pioneer as a member of the integrating class of Athens High School. It's hard to escape the fact that he encountered brutal racial slurs scrawled on the side of a building on the first day of school and yet endured, he said, without further incident. For him to return as one of the first athletic heroes to be honored by the school is a legacy many far more famous men would envy. He stood beside other legends of Athens, including Duke Carlisle, who went on to play quarterback for the University of Texas and led the Longhorns to their first national championship in 1963.

However, what made the night special were the people who were there for Tommy. Of course, Jackie stood proudly by his side in an elegant maroon dress (the primary school color of Athens). Tommy II helped direct friends and family to their seats and organized group photos. Bowman's older sister, Johnny, sat beside him at one of the head tables. Aunt Lynda, better known as "Poochie," who was a key member of the original core group that included her sister Alice, Tommy, and their cousin William, brought an extra dose of glamor to the occasion.

David Sibley and Tom Stanton attended, representing Bowman's Baylor teammates and the group that has stayed lifelong friends. They shared a table with Dr. Jimmy Hunter, Tommy's pastor.

Carroll Dawson was there with his wife, Sharon. It certainly didn't go unnoticed or unrecognized that Dawson had returned to the town where he made the now-famous discovery of the Athens High School senior.

Toni Clay wears many hats in Athens, Texas. She's Athens ISD's communications coordinator, along with serving as the town's mayor. As the Hall of Fame ceremony emcee, Clay held talk-show-esque question-and-answer sessions with each of the inductees. In introducing Bowman, she retold the story—taken almost directly from

Baylor's 1969–70 press guide—about how Granville Crayton told Dawson about the best basketball player in the state who resided in Athens.

The best story of the night, however, involved a small placard at Bowman's head table. He asked Clay if they could make a reserved-seat card for his mother, Irene Barker, who is deceased. Bowman explained that his mother worked in the kitchen at Athens Country Club and served tables in the dining room. So, on that night, he wanted her to have her own place designated to honor her memory in that way.

Bowman was one of four individuals who entered the Athens ISD Hall of Fame on that night as original members. They were joined by a couple of state championship golf teams. The evening was part roast, part storytelling-in-the-round. Sentimentality, for the most part, gave way to lightheartedness.

During his time on stage, Bowman joked about how Stanton got the nickname "Mad Dog." He recounted his college plans that were redirected by Dawson and informally recognized many of the people who had come to celebrate with him. He didn't have to give a formal speech, though he likely would have nailed it if he had. The occasion lacked heavy-handed seriousness. It had small-town comfort. And it wrapped up in well under two hours.

But Bowman made sure he once again gave credit where he always has.

"It was providence," Bowman said. "It was all about God, and it still is all about God."

Tommy Bowman looks to pass during a game against SMU.

Courtesy of the Texas Collection

Appendix

*Tommy Bowman's Baylor-Era Results
and Career Basketball Statistics*

Baylor's Bowman-Era Results

1967–68

December 1	Austin College	W	90–61
December 4	at Centenary	W	93–78
December 5	at Southwestern Louisiana	L	80–70
December 9	Tulane	W	93–82
December 12	Loyola New Orleans	W	88–75
December 19	Texas–Arlington	W	92–74
December 22	Oklahoma City	L	83–75
December 27	*Alabama	L	85–75
December 28	*Spring Hill	W	73–72
January 3	at SMU	W	76–66
January 6	Texas Tech	W	64–50
January 9	Arkansas	W	80–69
January 25	Tarleton State	W	101–67

January 27	at TCU	L	99–86
January 30	Rice	W	70–52
February 3	at Texas A&M	W	77–67
February 6	Texas	W	74–58
February 10	at Rice	W	59–58
February 13	at Texas	L	79–65
February 17	Texas A&M	L	67–63
February 20	SMU	L	70–63
February 24	at Texas Tech	L	65–63
February 27	at Arkansas	W	71–64
March 2	TCU	L	72–65

Mobile Classic (Mobile, Alabama)

1968–69

December 3	Texas Lutheran	W	73–52
December 6	at Loyola New Orleans	W	99–88
December 7	at Tulane	W	82–80
December 14	New Mexico State	L	69–58
December 20	*Hawaii	W	78–69
December 21	*Southwestern Louisiana	L	86–78
December 26	^William & Mary	W	81–68
December 27	^Virginia Tech	W	66–63
December 28	^Virginia	W	79–61
January 7	SMU	W	69–67
January 10	at TCU	W	68–64
January 23	Tarleton State	W	103–57
January 25	Texas Tech	L	73–70
January 28	at Arkansas	W	74–72
February 1	at Rice	W	71–68

February 4	Texas A&M	W	66–65
February 8	at Texas	W	71–57
February 11	Rice	L	75–73
February 15	Texas	W	63–58
February 18	at Texas A&M	L	86–74
February 22	at SMU	W	90–78 (OT)
February 25	TCU	L	70–66
March 1	Arkansas	W	66–54
March 4	at Texas Tech	W	65–63

Bayou Holiday Classic (Lafayette, Louisiana)

^East Carolina Classic (Greenville, North Carolina)

1969–70

December 2	Texas Wesleyan	W	89–49
December 6	at New Mexico State	L	102–83
December 8	at Arizona	L	81–76
December 11	Texas–Arlington	W	98–79
December 13	Southwestern Louisiana	W	95–68
December 19	*South Dakota	W	95–75
December 20	*New Mexico State	W	87–73
December 22	at Centenary	L	78–74 (OT)
December 30	Centenary	W	86–60
January 2	Wyoming	W	86–79
January 5	Texas	W	81–59
January 10	at Texas A&M	W	79–71
January 24	Arkansas	W	110–79
January 27	Texas Tech	W	47–46
January 31	at TCU	L	90–71
February 3	SMU	W	83–81 (OT)

February 7	at Rice	L	72–71
February 10	at Arkansas	L	76–75
February 14	Rice	L	61–60
February 17	at SMU	L	70–66
February 21	TCU	W	92–81
February 24	at Texas	L	81–70
February 28	Texas A&M	W	70–68
March 3	at Texas Tech	W	80–72

Cowboy Classic (Abilene, Texas)

Tommy Bowman's Career Basketball Statistics

	GAMES	FGM-FGA	PCT	FTM-FTA	PCT	REB	RPG	PTS	PPG
*1966–67	12	76–161	.472	42–61	.689	153	12.8	194	16.2
1967–68	24	123–251	.490	78–98	.796	225	9.4	324	13.5
1968–69	24	126–285	.442	114–138	.826	261	10.9	366	15.3
1969–70	24	97–234	.414	81–103	.786	209	8.7	275	11.5
Varsity Total (1967–70)	72	346–770	.449	273–339	.805	695	9.65	965	13.4

*freshman season

Printed in the USA
CPSIA information can be obtained
at www.ICGtesting.com
LVHW052009120124
768844LV00004B/321